Helion & Company Limited
Unit 8 Amherst Business Centre
Budbrooke Road
Warwick
CV34 5WE
England
Tel. 01926 499 619
Email: info@helion.co.uk
Website: www.helion.co.uk
Twitter: @helionbooks
Visit our blog http://blog.helion.co.uk/

Designed & typeset by Farr out Publications, Wokingham, Berkshire
Cover design by Paul Hewitt, Battlefield Design (www.battlefi eld-design.co.uk)

ISBN 978-1-914059-23-0

British Library Cataloguing-in-Publication Data
A catalogue record for this book is available from the British Library

We always welcome receiving book proposals from prospective authors.

CONTENTS

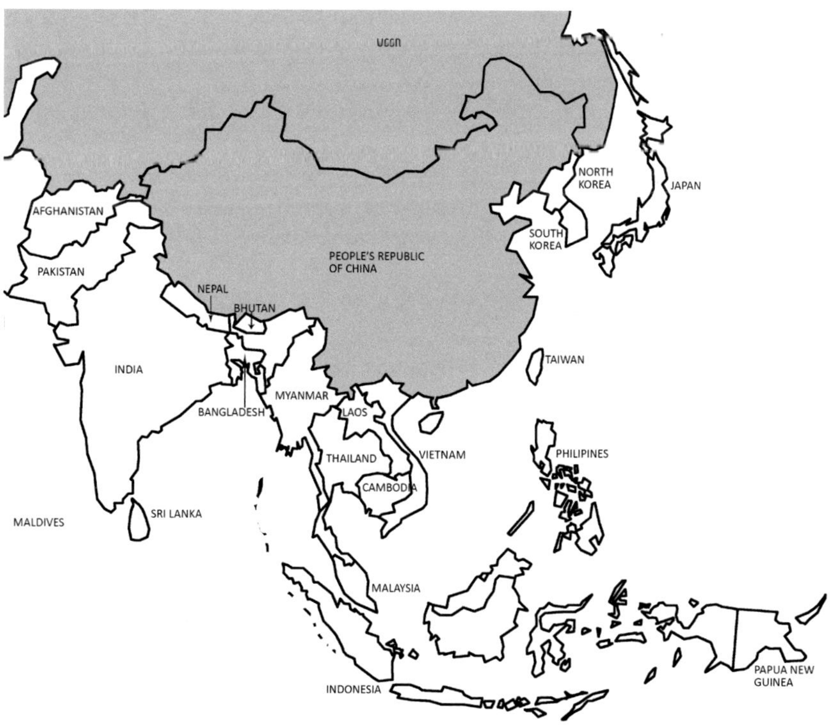

Note: In order to simplify the use of this book, all names, locations and geographic designations are as provided in *The Times World Atlas*, or other traditionally accepted major sources of reference, as of the time of described events.

ABBREVIATIONS

APC	armoured personnel carrier
CC CPSU	Central Committee of the Communist Party of the Soviet Union
CPC	Communist Party of China
GDR	German Democratic Republic
PLA	People's Liberation Army of China
PRC	People's Republic of China
RSFSR	Russian Soviet Federalist Socialist Republic

ACKNOWLEDGEMENTS

We would like to express our sincere thanks to the veterans who directly took part in the events of 1969: A.D. Konstantinov, Yu.V. Babansky, N.I. Popov, V.D. Pavlyuk, N.A. Zadorozhny, G.M. Zhestkov, A.V. Shamov, V.M. Tirskikh, A.I. Nikitin, N.A. Rozhkov, V.V. Puchkov, Ye.B. Govor, A.A. Murzin, and A.I. Tsogla. These men agreed to meet and talk personally or entered into fruitful correspondence with the authors.

We thank the directors of the Foundation for the Support of Veterans of the Border Guards, 'Vernost', and also the directors of the Central Border Museum of the Federal Security Service of the Russian Federation for permission to use their photo archives.

We would like to express our appreciation to A.A. Sabadash, Ye.D. Leonova, O.N. Bykova, V.N. Volik, S.P. Vashenyak, A.L. Volkov, A.D. Leonkin, A.N. Musalov, V.I. Gladkov, G.V. Kravchenko, D.V. Kiselev, Reiko Nishioka (Japan), and Elizabeth McGuire (USA) for the materials they provided.

Several citizens of the People's Republic of China rendered generous assistance in the work on this book, selflessly providing many Chinese materials. Complying with their request, we will not identify them by name; nevertheless, we wish to express our sincere gratitude to them.

The Authors

TO THE READERS OF THE ENGLISH-LANGUAGE EDITION

I was 12 years old when the newspapers reported about the fighting on the Sino-Soviet border. Although this happened long ago, I still remember the fear that gripped me: it seemed from one day to the next that a very real war would begin, the kind of war that my father, who knew well what war meant, remembered.

The newspapers at that time were full of reports from the border, but it was difficult to make sense of what was actually happening there. As far as I now understand, the Soviet mass media did not assign itself the task of clarifying the details of the fighting that had erupted: the main thing was to use the moment to rally the people around the leadership of the USSR.

Time passed. My interest in the events of 1969 had not faded, but there was no opportunity to find out anything new. The mass media quickly forgot about what had happened, and my attempts to familiarize myself with archival materials were in vain. Only with the appearance of the internet did I understand that the time had come to satisfy my own curiosity.

Inasmuch as my experience in applying to official authorities was unsuccessful, I decided to seek out veterans of the events so as to reconstitute, with their help, an actual picture of what had happened. This idea was exceptionally fruitful: I was able to personally meet or correspond with many veterans, diplomats, special services officers, relatives of those who died, historians and others. As it turned out, many of them had kept documentary evidence about the fighting on the border, which they shared with me. I cannot say that the work was easy, inasmuch as over the years much had been forgotten or had become distorted in the memory of the eyewitnesses. It was necessary to compare their recollections on the subject for compliance in the description of various details, and even to take into account the human weakness of wanting to embellish one's own participation in events. With time, I was able to familiarize myself with publications on this theme by Chinese and foreign authors; this enriched the general picture with new details.

The book, *The Sino-Soviet Border War of 1969*, is the result of my 20 years of work on this subject. It is possible that even now the text may contain some small errors and inaccuracies; however, this is completely normal for any historical research. There is, however, a question that I would like to immediately clarify. I am talking about objectivity, which the foreign reader has a right to expect from any author. Inasmuch as I am a citizen of Russia, someone may have doubts as to my ability to look at the events of 1969 through the eyes of an impartial researcher. I would like to make two comments on this matter:

First, when reading the works of various historians I noticed many times that their understanding of objectivity consists of laying equal responsibility for what happened on each of the opposing sides. If one of the sides is accused of something, an accusation of the same gravity is immediately lodged against the other side – for balance, so to speak. I do not acknowledge the objectivity of this approach to the analysis of historical events. Of course, there are situations when both sides are guilty, for example, the history of the advent of the ideological discussion between the Communist Party of the Soviet Union and the Communist Party of China in the second half of the 1950s. If, however, it is a matter of the employment of weapons, then one cannot talk about equal blame, inasmuch as it does not happen that shooting begins simultaneously from both sides. Furthermore, if fire was opened by surprise, according to a plan that had been developed earlier, then it should be clearly pointed out who organized the bloodshed; there should be no attempts to justify those who are guilty by citing some political or psychological motives.

Second, my relationship with Russian scholarly journals is not very good. Only two of my articles on this issue have been published in Russia, and those were edited, which did not make them any better. The majority of my work has been published in the US and Japan, the reason being that the editors of Russian journals are not free to select materials for publication. They only obediently follow the current government line of barring any painful discussions about the history of relations with China. Many times I had to hear from editors the "But who needs this?", "Why stir up the past?", "The article is interesting, but we will not publish it, we are now strengthening fraternal relations with China", etc. explanations of rejection. Someone even warned me that there would be trouble for me if I continued to work on this subject.

The policy of silence about the events of 1969, which is now being cultivated in Russia and China, has an extremely undesirable trend as its consequence – the presentation of the border war in two versions: the Soviet/Russian one and the Chinese one. This is a very convenient position for falsifiers and irresponsible loudmouths of all stripes: they say that the Russians say one thing and the Chinese another, and no one knows how it really was. The correct formulation of the issue is that there is always only one truth, and truth has no national affiliation. In the final analysis, everything depends on whether a researcher tries to get to the bottom of the truth or cravenly and dishonestly follows the instructions of official authorities.

My long study of the subject of the 1969 border war is not part of some project and has not been tailored to conform to conclusions and assessments that were made earlier. I carefully delved into what happened first and foremost for me, inasmuch as I was sincerely curious about what happened at that time on the border. I cannot rationally explain this interest. It is simply interesting – that is the whole explanation.

In conclusion, I would like to say a few words about my co-author, Doctor H. Orenstein. His contribution to the work on this book was invaluable. Not only did the entire translation of the Russian text into English fall completely on his shoulders, but his knowledge of military terminology and the issue itself of the events on the Sino-Soviet border in 1969 was also extremely important. His advice made it possible to make the book more logical and accessible not only to specialists, but also to the broadest circle of readers interested in military history. I am therefore very grateful to him for his participation in this joint work.

I would be very interested in the opinions of those who read this book. For those who would like to comment, my e-mail address is: dmitry_ryabushkin@mail.ru.

D.S. Ryabushkin

1
HISTORY OF THE PROBLEM

As a rule, any research of the Sino-Soviet Border War of 1969 begins with an account of the history of the border demarcation between Russia/the USSR and China/People's Republic of China (PRC). There is no reason to break with that tradition.

Sources available to researchers attest that the border between Russia and China had not been determined as a result of wars or large-scale conflicts. Of course, clashes and misunderstandings took place, but they were more of a local character and, therefore, could not poison the historical memory of the Russians and Chinese with deep-felt mutual animosity.

Sometime, at the dawn of the establishment of mutual relations between Russia and China, vast territories stretched between the two countries – mostly sparsely populated (sometimes even unpopulated) taiga and semi-desert areas. China's northern border was the Great Wall, defending it from the Amur and Ussuri Rivers for more than 1,000 kilometres. The Chinese built this wall over the course of several centuries to protect their country from nomad invasions.

Russian settlements appeared in the Amur region in the first half of the 17th century, when Manchuria was a state that was separate from China, populated by representatives of a special ethnic group – the Manchurians. At that time the Manchurians were stronger than the Chinese: in 1644 they captured Peking and imposed the rule of the Qing Dynasty upon them. China lost its independence and became part of the Manchurian state. As late as the end of the 19th century Manchuria was a special entity on whose territory the rights of the Chinese were restricted: they were forbidden to settle and farm here.

At the end of the 17th century the Manchurian emperors organised several campaigns against the Russian settlements on the Amur, and for some time held this new territory of theirs. Manchurian rulers also made conquests in Mongolia, Eastern Turkestan, and other neighbouring lands.

The border established between Russia and China has its own special history, in which there have been more than a few curious twists, secrets, and minor tragedies and comedies. A total of around 40 documents exist that are directly associated with this problem, but only seven of them had serious consequences:

1) The Treaty of Nerchinsk (6 September 1689) was the first treaty between Russia and the Qing Empire, which very roughly established the borders. It contributed to the organisation of trade and diplomatic relations between Russia and China. In accordance with the treaty, Russia ceded the Amur *Oblast* to China.
2) The Burinsky Treaty (31 August 1727) determined the Sino-Russian border from the Shabin-Dabat Pass (Western Sayan) to the Argun River (Abagaytu Hill area). The articles became part of the Treaty of Kyakhta.
3) The Treaty of Kyakhta (1 November 1727) registered agreements between Russia and China. It clarified the overall border and established a procedure for contacts of the border authorities and determined border posts for Sino-Russian trade. It permitted Russian caravans to access Peking once every three years and gave the Russian spiritual mission in Peking the status of unofficial permanent representation in China.

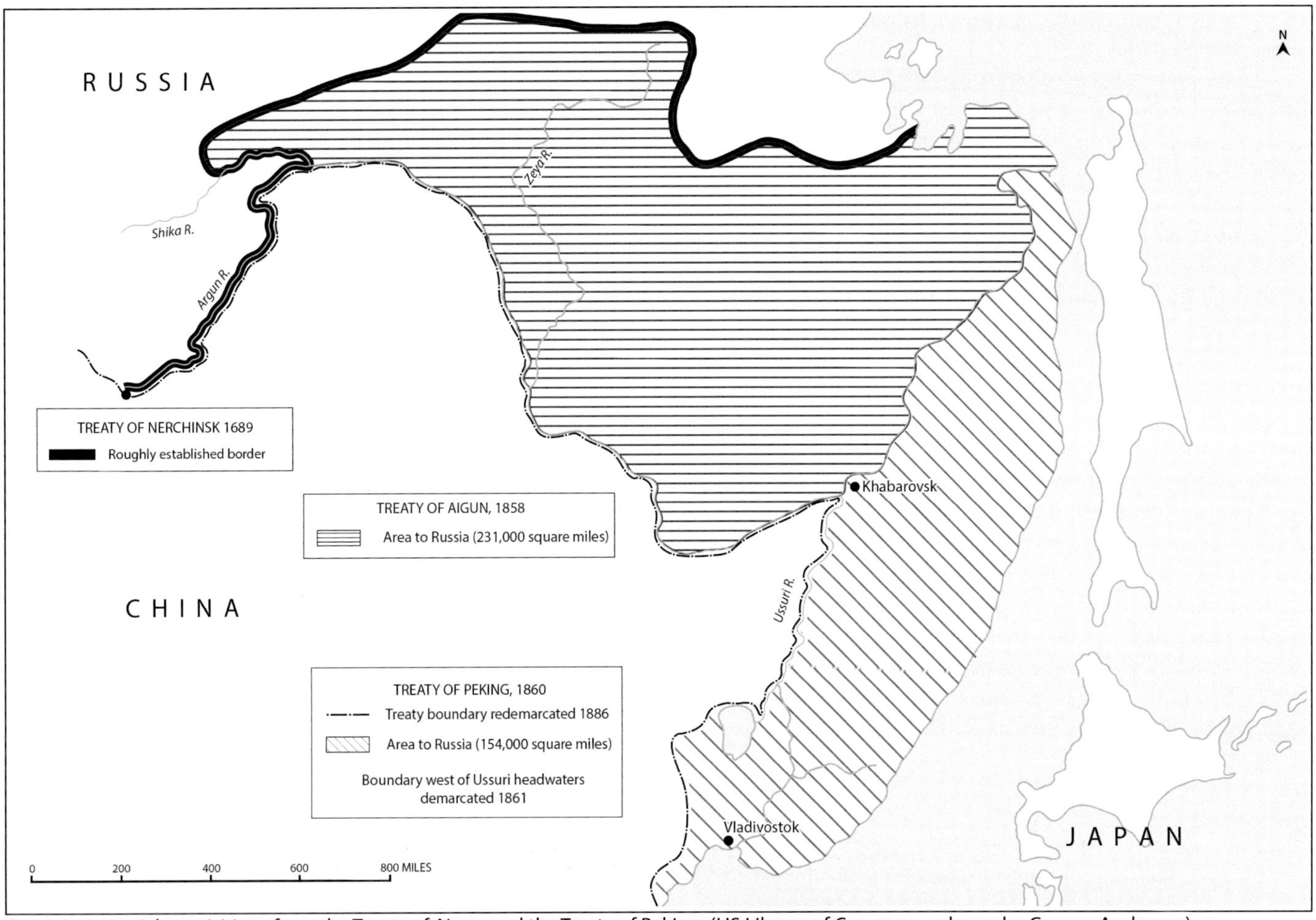

Russia's territorial acquisitions from the Treaty of Aigun and the Treaty of Peking. (US Library of Congress, redrawn by George Anderson)

4) The Treaty of Aigun (28 May 1858) returned the Amur *Oblast* to Russia. Territories on the left bank of the Amur, from the Argun River to the Sea of Okhotsk, were given to Russia and the Ussuri *Krai* was acknowledged to be a joint possession of Russia and China. Russian and Chinese ships were allowed free navigation on the Amur, Ussuri, and Songhua Rivers.
5) The Sino-Russian Treaty of Tianjin (13 June 1858) broadened Russia's political and commercial rights in China. It envisioned the determination of parts of the border between Russia and China that had not been established at that time.
6) The Treaty of Peking (14 November 1860) was a supplement and completion of the 1858 Treaties of Aigun and Tianjin. It established the eastern border between Russia and China along the Amur, Ussuri, and Song'acha Rivers, and secured for Russia the Amur *Krai* and Ussuri *Krai*.
7) The Treaty of Petersburg (24 February 1881) transferred the Iliysk *Krai* (with the exclusion of a small area) to China, clarified the border in the Lake Zaysan region and the Black Irtysh River, and determined the procedure for resolving border issues.

The first of the above-mentioned treaties was very unfavourable for Russia. In fact, it was signed under the threat of the employment of force, inasmuch as a Manchurian-Chinese force numbering several thousand confronted the Russian embassy and a detachment of several hundred men. It was, however, also a positive moment: from that time Russia actively traded its traditionally exported goods with China, receiving in exchange tea, silk, and porcelain.

With regard to the Sino-Soviet Border War, the 1860 Treaty of Peking is the most often cited of the above-mentioned seven treaties. In fact, its signing was a kind of result in the development of relations between Russia and China. The value of the 1860 treaty, however, is determined by the fact that it confirmed two previous agreements – the Treaty of Aigun and the Treaty of Tianjin.[1]

The first of these was the result of negotiations conducted between Governor-General of Eastern Siberia N.N. Muravyev and the Chinese emperor's representative Yi Shan in May 1858. Many, many years later the Chinese Communist leadership called this treaty unequal; however, the participants in the negotiations considered it differently. At least the preamble of the Treaty of Aigun stated that the sides signed it 'by common agreement, thanks to the eternal mutual friendship between the two states, for the good of their subjects.'

It is completely natural to ask the question: Was the declared 'common agreement' not a step that was forced on the Chinese government? This question should be answered affirmatively, inasmuch as at this time China was undergoing difficult times in connection with the Second Opium War and the Taiping Rebellion. Had the Chinese acted otherwise, they would have had one more conflict on their northern borders. At the same time, it should be stressed that Russia had not achieved the above-mentioned 'common agreement' by means of war or a military threat. The Chinese themselves had made their choice, based on internal considerations.

The Treaty of Tianjin was signed in Tianjin by Russian Commissar in China E.V. Putyatin and Chinese plenipotentiary Hua Shan. It envisioned the establishment of responsible groups of researchers, who would study the situation in place and negotiate the border line. This document stated: 'Upon the designation of the borders, a detailed description and maps will be made of the adjacent areas,

N.P. Ignatyev. (unknown photographer)

which in the future will also serve as indisputable documents about the borders for both governments.'

Inasmuch as the Treaty of Aigun did not demarcate the lands from the Ussuri to the sea, the Russian government sent a special mission to Peking, headed by Count N.P. Ignatyev, for further negotiations. 'Prince Gong, known as Yi Xing,' took part in the negotiations for the Chinese.

This time the matter proceeded with more difficulty, because the Chinese had won a number of victories over the English and French, and, therefore, were feeling surer of themselves. However, the defeats of the Western allies were only temporary, and quite soon the Anglo-French forces were at the gates of Peking.

Circumstances prompted the Chinese diplomats to agree with Ignatyev's recommendations, and they signed a new treaty, the Treaty of Peking.[2] As both negotiating sides affirmed, this document was accepted '…for the greater bolstering of the mutual friendship between the two empires, for the development of trade relations, and for the prevention of misunderstandings.'

In 1861 a protocol about the exchange of maps and descriptions of the demarcations was attached to this treaty as one of its components. P.V. Kozakevich and K.F. Budogossky signed the protocol for the Russians, and Cheng Qi and Jing Chun signed for the Chinese. In addition, the protocol was sealed with official stamps.

Prince Gong. (unknown photographer)

A clarification of the question of how the border was drawn on the maps attached to the Treaty of Peking is extremely important. And so, the border was drawn by a red line mainly along the Chinese bank of the Amur and Ussuri Rivers and along the Amur Canal. Here and there the red line passed directly through the islands, dividing them into a Russian section and a Chinese section; some islands were entirely given to China. On the whole, the above-mentioned rivers mostly belonged to Russia.

Was this demarcation fair? Definitely not, for one cannot consider the situation fair when a river between two states is divided clearly in favor of one of the sides. However, even the most unfair treaty must be executed if the two sides have signed it. Any inequities in such issues can be corrected with the help of negotiations and the subsequent conclusion of a new treaty. Of course, however, there is another variant – War.

History knows instances where a river border was drawn along the riverbank of one of the states. International law allows for this possibility in the case where such a demarcation occurred for historical reasons, either in accordance with a treaty or because one of the sides colonised the second riverbank before the neighbouring side began to colonise it. A general rule was and is to draw the border along the thalweg (line of greatest depth) of the main channel of navigable rivers and along the middle of non-navigable rivers.[3] On the other hand, it should be made clear that there also existed no firmly established and obligatory principle for drawing a border along the thalweg of a main channel. Rather, it was a question of a rule, acknowledged by the majority of states, according to which drawing the border along a channel was fair, correct, and not subject to dispute in the future.

In contemporary literature (including Russian), there are sometimes statements that dispute the ownership of the islands on the Amur and Ussuri Rivers. Moreover, at one time some Russian officials – for example, from the Ministry of Foreign Affairs – adhered to the same opinion. The logic of the authors of such 'discoveries' was approximately this: the supposed length of the border between China and Russia, the complex relief of the terrain, and the natural

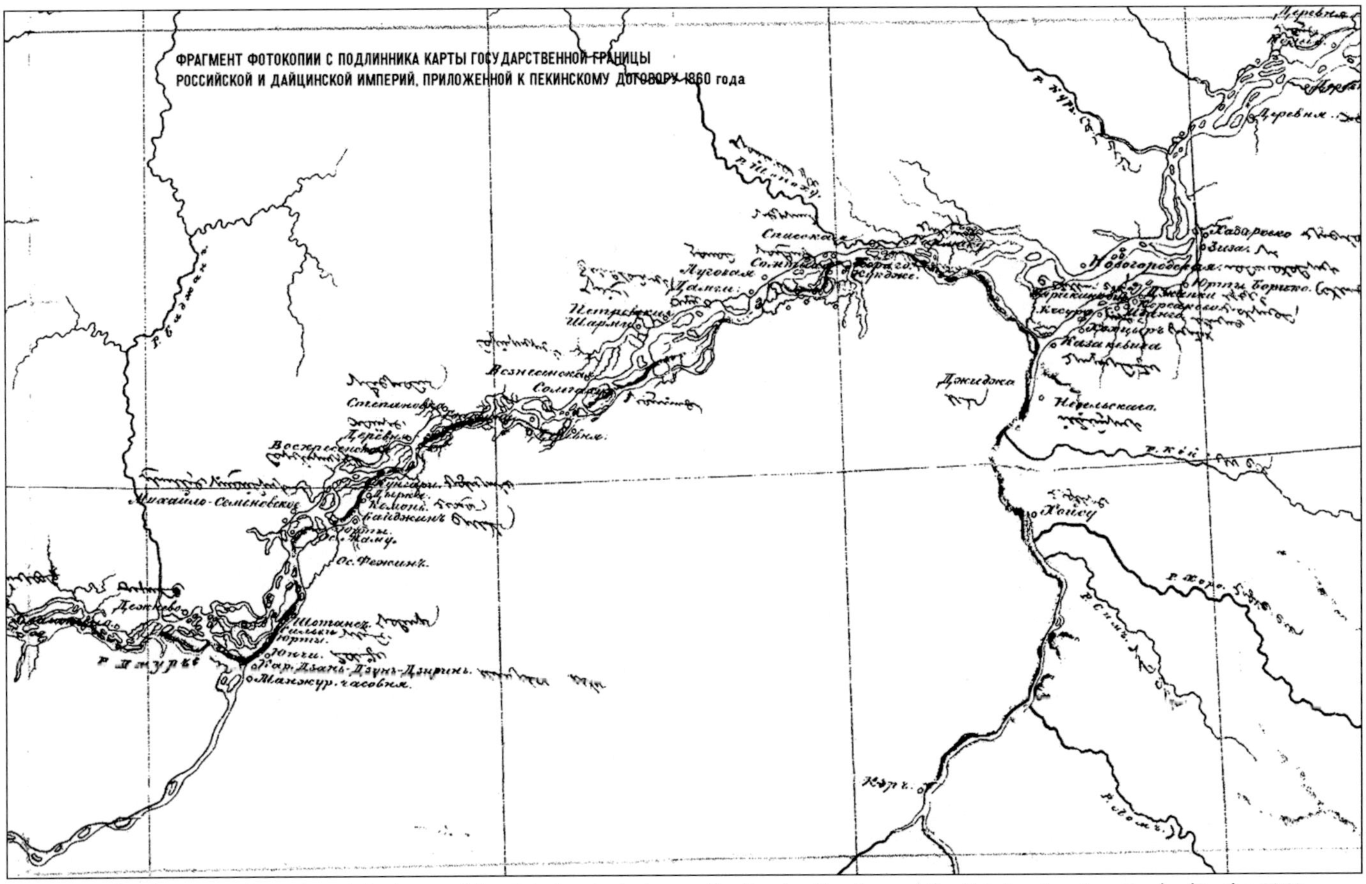

Fragment of a photocopy from the original map of the state border between the Russian Empire and the Daiqing Empire, attached to the 1860 Treaty of Peking. (provided by A.D. Leonkin)

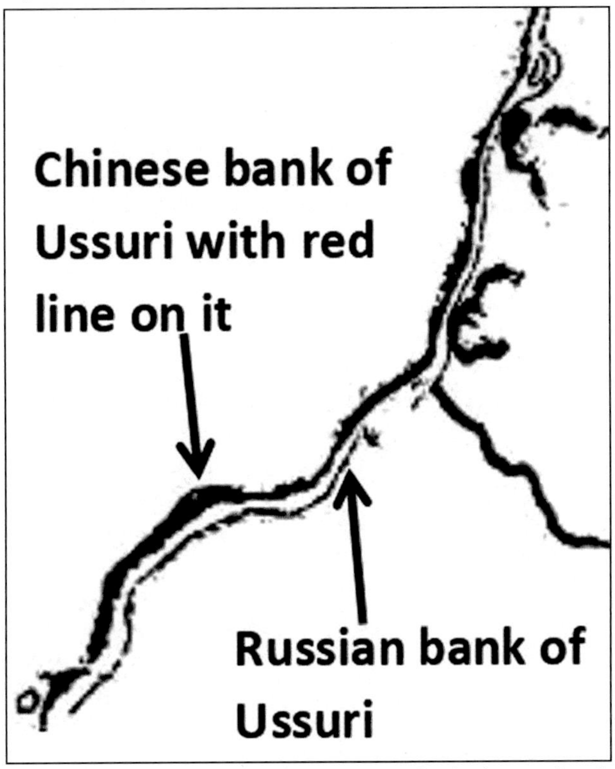

An enlarged section of the preceding map. It is clearly obvious that the red line runs directly along the Chinese bank of the Ussuri.

and climatic features resulted in the absence of a precise line of demarcation between the two countries. This particularly concerned those sectors where the border ran along rivers. In general, they say, the islands on the rivers were never demarcated, nor were their territorial affiliation determined.

In the 2002 (No. 6) issue of *Otechestvennye zapiski* (Domestic Notes) the same ideas were presented as follows:

> The sources of the conflict lie in the inadequacy of the conditions of the Treaty of Peking, 14 November 1860, according to which the area and islands were not demarcated; the borderline that was kept had developed historically, and in a number of sectors was disputed by China. Damansky Island was located nearer to the Chinese side from the main channel of the river (approximately 40 metres from the riverbank), and China laid claim to it.[4]

Leonid Mitrofanovich Zamyatin, who in 1969 was Chief of the Press Department of the USSR Ministry of Foreign Affairs (MFA) and who did much to correctly inform the world community about events on the border, also completely confused the essence of the issue. Here is what he said about the problem of the disputed territory:

> In our opinion, such a problem simply did not exist. On all maps compiled even 100 years ago, the river border between Russia and China ran along the main channel of the Amur and Ussuri Rivers. Not along the middle of the rivers, but along their deepest place. And the islands north of the main channel were always considered to be Russian. But here, unexpectedly for us, the Chinese had laid claim to a group of eternally flooded Ussuri islands, including Damansky Island.[5]

One would like to know: On which maps did the border between Russia and China 'run along the main channel'? If we have in mind the Treaty of Peking, then the border mainly runs along the Chinese riverbank, and not along the main channel.

Further, which islands lie 'north of the main channel'? If it is a question of the Amur, then it is understood. But the Ussuri River flows from south to north, and, therefore, its main channel divides the river islands into western and eastern.

Furthermore, why was this Chinese claim 'unexpected' for the Soviet leadership? After all, the arrival of citizens from the PRC to the Soviet islands had been going on for almost 10 years; conflicts and skirmishes had continuously arisen. Nevertheless 'unexpectedly'?

In general, regarding the version of uncertainty about the status of the islands on the Sino-Soviet border, one can state the following consideration: it is possible that the author collective of the cited treatment was a propaganda apparatus of the Chinese Communist Party, to which the Chinese political leadership had given the task of 'scientifically' justifying claims to Soviet territory. The above-cited Russian authors and diplomats, for reasons that cannot be understood, mindlessly repeated the fabrications of the Peking ideologues.

After the October Revolution, Lenin's government in Russia annulled the unequal and secret treaties that had been concluded by tsarist authority with other states.

On 25 July 1919, the government of the Russian Soviet Federalist Socialist Republic (RSFSR) turned to the Chinese people and the Chinese leadership at that time with explanations as to what specifically the treaties had in mind. Among these were enumerated all agreements about China's spheres of influence, extraterritorial laws, concessions, and indemnities. Sino-Soviet border agreements were not, however, included in this list, inasmuch as the government of the RSFSR did not consider them to be unequal.

At the end of the 1920s, Chinese society entered into an era of severe trials. First the destruction of the bourgeois-democratic revolution, and then the occupation of north-eastern China by Japanese forces led to a certain tension on the border. The Soviets were completely justified in suspecting the Japanese militarists of aggressive intentions, and took measures to strengthen its borders. Thus, in 1935 the General Staff of the Red Army published topographic maps on which the 'red line' signified the state border of the USSR. It should be mentioned for the sake of fairness that Japanese forces acknowledged this border and, on the whole, did not attempt to seize any Soviet territories near the border rivers. Japanese officials also did not raise the issue of changing the situation that had developed. Here is a characteristic example. At the end of 1932 troops of Chinese General Su Bingwen crossed the Soviet border and put themselves at the disposal of Soviet authorities; the Japanese pursuing them stopped at the Soviet border.

Of course, some problems were, nevertheless, unavoidable, inasmuch as relations at that time between Japan and the USSR were rather far from friendly. The fact is that even in tsarist times the attitude of the Russian authorities toward the arrival of local Chinese on the islands was quite liberal, inasmuch as the latter were involved in purely agricultural activities – mowing grass, collecting firewood, etc. Naturally, there was no hint of politics here, and the Russians turned a blind eye to such border violations. The Japanese took advantage of this situation and, on the heels of the local inhabitants, sent armed soldiers to the islands. As a result, conflicts arose.

However, it was the Chinese Communists who began to express real dissatisfaction with the existing border, when in 1949 the People's Republic of China, headed by Mao Zedong, was formed.

The claims to the USSR did not appear immediately. For example, when in 1952 the Soviets sent a set of topographic maps to China, this was accepted with thanks. No one disputed the borderline that had been drawn on these maps, no one mentioned 'lost territories.' Incidentally, this term itself sounds strange, inasmuch as the history of any country is the history of continuous loss and acquisition of territory.

In the mid-1950s, the first signs appeared attesting to a change of position on the part of the Chinese. During one of the campaigns, which were carried out under the slogan, 'Let 100 flowers bloom, let 100 schools of thought contend', Chinese newspapers began to publish articles on the irregularities of the border question with the USSR. It is significant that Mao Zedong and other Chinese leaders continued in words to pledge eternal friendship with the Soviet people, but in deeds undertook no measures to halt such discussions.

Furthermore, the PRC's government publishers had already begun to publish maps that identified Soviet territories as having at one time been lost by China. Starting in 1960, hostility in relations with the USSR became open, and it was at this time that a long-term practice (lasting right up to 1969) of organising all kinds of provocations at the border began. In 1964 Mao pronounced his well-known phrase that has been cited innumerable times since then: 'Approximately 100 years ago the region east of Baikal became Russian territories, and since then Vladivostok, Khabarovsk, Kamchatka, and other points have been territory of the Soviet Union. We still have not submitted a bill for this list.'

There was no delay in submitting the bill: soon the Chinese leadership announced a list of claims: 1.5 million square kilometres of Soviet territory, including the cities of Khabarovsk, Vladivostok, Blagoveshchensk, and others. And in unofficial talks the Chinese spoke about 3 million square kilometres.

Once again it should be emphasized: when discussing the reasons for the Sino-Soviet armed conflict, many authors point to the irregularity of the border between the USSR and PRC. Moreover, specific people from the political leadership of the Soviet Union are named, although they are hardly personally responsible for what happened.

For example, the official publication of the Federal Border Service of Russia[6] mentioned talks on border issues that were conducted in 1964 between official representatives of the two countries.[7] General Colonel Pavel Ivanovich Zyryanov,[8] Commander of the Border Troops, headed the delegation; for the occasion he was appointed deputy minister of foreign affairs. Talks proceeded with difficulty, but finally they managed to negotiate almost all disputed issues. Thus, the sides agreed that the border on the rivers should run along the main channel. That being said, however, disagreements arose regarding the islands in the region of Khabarovsk, which the Chinese wished to see as their own. These islands (Tarabarov and Bolshoy Ussuriysky) were and are still very important; therefore, the Soviet delegation could not agree to transfer them to China. Nevertheless, they found a way out of this impasse: both sides agreed to postpone examining the issue of the status of the disputed islands for the future, while for the time being signing a treaty on the agreed sectors of the border.

The opinions of various authors differ as to what happened later. Some say that First Secretary of the Central Committee of the Communist Party of the Soviet Union (CC CPSU) N.S. Khrushchev, known for his impulsiveness (often changing into petty tyranny), took an 'all or nothing' position; as a result, no documents were signed. It is this fact that the advocates of this position cite as the main reason for the border war that arose. Other historians, however, lay the blame on Mao: supposedly Mao intentionally instigated a halt to the negotiations, having advanced claims to extensive Soviet territory.[9] According to this version, Khrushchev actually took a wise position, deciding to run the border along the main channel of the rivers, thereby removing the tension in relations between China and the USSR. Nikita Sergeyevich himself recalled these events:

> When the Chinese sent us their maps, we saw that ... they were presenting demands on those islands on the border rivers that were closer to the Chinese side than to the Soviet side. They proposed that we newly mark the borders: instead of running the border along the Chinese riverbank, it should run along the middle of the river. This proposal was in accordance with international practice; therefore, we agreed with it, although this also meant that we relinquished control of the majority of the islands ...
>
> When, in the final analysis, it came time to sign the border agreement, which had established new borders, we were ready to give up something and gain something ... However, what were sensible concessions for us turned out to be not good enough from the Chinese point of view. When our representatives returned to China for the final round of negotiations, the Chinese did not accept our positions... They wanted us to acknowledge that the currently existing borders were based on illegal and unfair treaties that the tsars had imposed on a weak Chinese government. They wanted our new treaty to include an article that would have indicated that the new borders were a continuation of the injustice imposed on China more than one hundred years ago. How could any sovereign government sign such a document?
>
> The talks broke off and our delegation returned home.[10]

It is difficult to say with certainty which version is the correct one. It is possible that they both are: after all, both could have happened without a large time gap. However it may have been, many researchers think the problem about the islands on the river was the main reason for the war.

Judging by everything, the advocates of this hypothesis muddle two concepts: cause and reason. The cause for any phenomenon has, as a rule, deep roots and it is not always understood by the public, simply because of the public's meagre knowledge. As for reason, it often, and very successfully, is masked by the cause, deceiving not only the broad public, but also professionals.

In order to understand that the border disputes played the role specifically of the reason, it is sufficient to briefly glimpse at the map: well really, can tiny islands on rivers and small elevations be the real cause for such a serious conflict between two great powers, which, moreover, possess nuclear weapons? For China and the USSR, with their enormous territories, what wedge of light converged on these scraps of land? It means that this was not a matter of border treaties, but of greater politics. If there had not been islands and elevations, the organisers of the bloodbath would have found another reason for the conflict.

After the first (March) fighting on the Ussuri River (Damansky Island), Soviet and Chinese officials began to correspond about whom the islands belonged to. The position of the Chinese was that the existing treaties about the border were unequal and, therefore, the Chinese did not consider themselves obliged to abide by them. Peking announced that Damansky Island 'is Chinese territory,' and the Ussuri River 'was an interior river of China' before the signing of the Treaty of Peking.

In this respect, it makes sense to repeat once again that the Chinese themselves sealed themselves off from the external world with the Great Wall, thereby designating the border of their presence. The Manchurians lived to the north, a distance of 800 kilometres and more from the Amur and Ussuri Rivers.

Researchers of Chinese history know well terms such as 'willow palisade': this was a line of fortifications built by the Manchurians to mark the northern border of their domain. Now then, this line ran near Mukden (Manchurian for what is today Shenyang). Thus, in 1969 and later the Chinese were clearly attempting to twist the facts of history.

To sum up, one can thus specify the positions of the sides. The Chinese leadership considered the many treaties about the borders with their neighbours to have been forced upon them and to be unequal, and, therefore, subject to change. The Soviets were ready to adjust the borderline, but only on the basis of acknowledging all signed treaties.

The position of the Soviet leadership was very specifically formulated in an announcement by the government on 13 June 1969:

> The Soviets support the following: to establish a consensus regarding border sectors for which there are no disagreements; with regard to individual sectors where there are disagreements, to come to an understanding of where the borderline runs by means of mutual consultations on the basis of treaties; with regard to sectors that are subject to natural changes, to proceed from treaties that are in force when determining the borderline, observing the principle of mutual concessions and the economic interests of the local population in these sectors; to fix an agreement, with both sides signing the appropriate documents.[11]

The Sino-Soviet Border War began on 2 March 1969 on Damansky Island, which became a symbol of the enmity between the USSR and China.

Russian researchers say that the island had been named in honour of Stanislav Ignatyevich Damansky, a Russian engineer-track layer who worked on an exploratory expedition.[12] The expedition was headed by A.P. Ursati, and its task was to reconnoitre the terrain in the interests of the railroad department.

Damansky died in 1888, when he attempted to cross the Ussuri by boat with two soldiers. Several days after the tragic occurrence, the river gave up the engineer's body to the island. It was then that the members of the expedition decided to name the island Damansky in memory of their colleague.

However, some contemporary Chinese historians point out that the island was formed on the Ussuri River only in 1915; before that it had presented itself as a protrusion of the Chinese riverbank. The river water allegedly washed away the connecting piece of land, and after this a new island appears on maps, connected with the shore, as before, by an underwater spit.

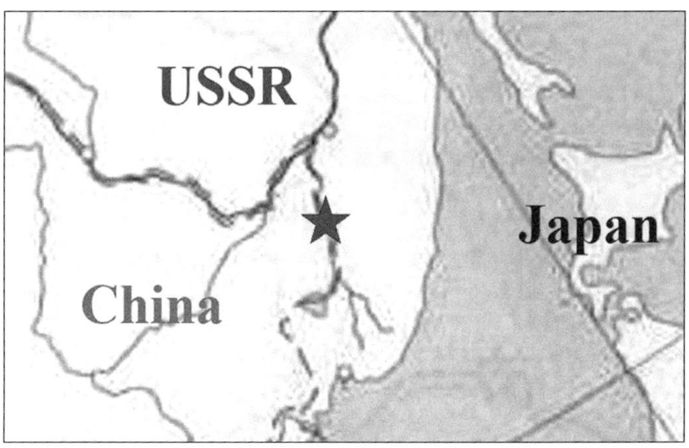

Location of Damansky Island on the map (indicated by a star). (authors' inscriptions on the contour of the map)

It is easy to note that there is a certain contradiction between the romantic version of the naming and the Chinese statements about when the island was formed. This contradiction can be easily removed if a map of Damansky Island dated before 1915 is made public. Undoubtedly, such a map exists in the archives; therefore, one can only complain about the archives not being accessible to the public.

Nonetheless, the Russian point of view is the more validated. The fact is that Soviet notes and announcements immediately after the war spoke about where the 'red line' ran in the region of the island along the Chinese riverbank. The Chinese did not refute this statement, thereby silently acknowledging that Damansky Island belonged to Russia. Had it been otherwise, the Chinese would surely have used this fact as their trump card.

At the end of the 1960s Damansky Island was located in the Pozharsky District of Primorsky *Krai*, bordering the Chinese county of Hulin in Heilongjiang Province. In order to orient oneself on a map, one can draw a parallel through the town of Luchegorsk (Primorsky *Krai*): where it intersects with the Sino-Russian border is approximately where Damansky is located.

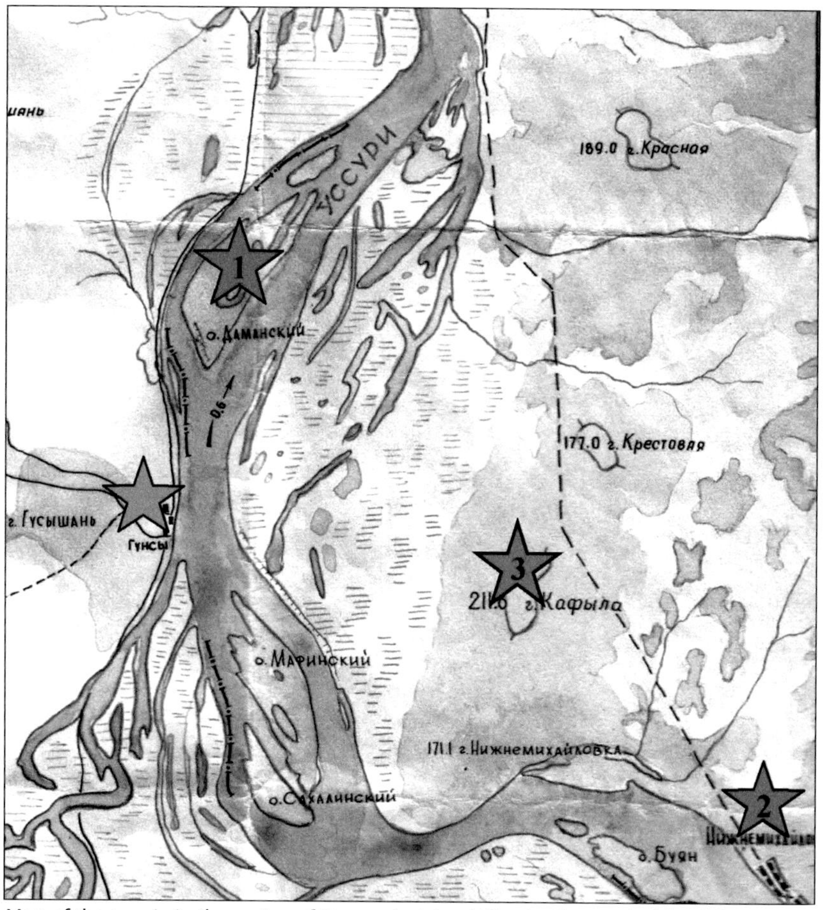

Map of the terrain in the region of Damansky Island. Star 1 – Damansky Island; Star 2 – the Soviet 2nd Border Outpost; Star 3 – the Soviet observation post; unnumbered star – the Chinese outpost. (provided by A. I. Nikitin)

From the Soviet riverbank to the island was an average of around 500 metres (in the order of 260 metres at its narrowest spot); from the Chinese riverbank – around 300 metres (in the order of 130 metres at its narrowest spot). Damansky stretches 1,700 metres from south to north, and its width is 500 metres. These numbers are rather approximate, inasmuch as the dimensions of the island depend on the time of year. For example, at the end of summer, when the typhoons and torrential rains come, the northern part of Damansky is flooded with water, while in winter the island rises as a dark mountain on the smooth, icy surface of the river.

In form, the island resembles a dolphin, although to the Chinese it recalls more a *yuanbao*, an ancient gold coin.

The vegetation on Damansky is represented mainly by the artisan willow and other trees. Several other islands are located in the immediate vicinity of Damansky: Kirkinsky Island (to the north) and Mafinsky Island, Sakhalinsky, and Buyan (all three to the south). In 1969 the border was such that all the islands belonged to the USSR.

Five mountain peaks could be seen on Damansky from the Soviet side: Ostraya (257 metres high), Krasnaya (189 metres), Krestovaya (177 metres), Kafyla (212 metres), and Nizhne-Mikhaylovka (171 metres). On the Chinese side were

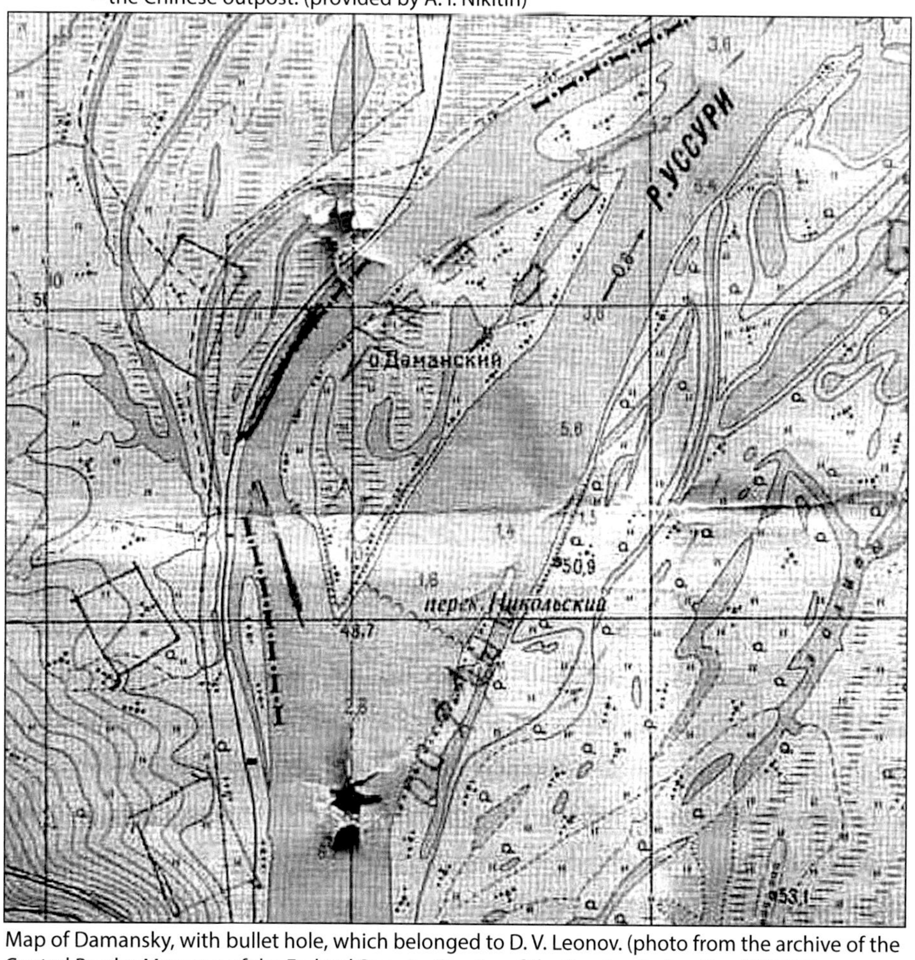

Map of Damansky, with bullet hole, which belonged to D. V. Leonov. (photo from the archive of the Central Border Museum of the Federal Security Service of the Russian Federation [FSB RF])

The village of Nizhne-Mikhaylovka, where Border Outpost No. 2 of the Iman Border Detachment was located. (photo© The Khabarovsk Territorial Museum after N.I. Grodekov)

Beigongsishan (150 metres), Dongshitoushan (353 metres) and Gusishan (209 metres).

Territorially, Damansky Island belonged to the sector of the border that was guarded by the 2nd Border Outpost (Nizhne-Mikhaylovka) of the Ussuri Border Detachment.[13] The outpost was located six kilometres as the crow flies, south of the island. At the time of the initial incidents in 1967–1969, Senior Lieutenant Ivan Ivanovich Strelnikov was in command of the outpost[14] and his deputy for political affairs was Junior Lieutenant Mikhail Illarionovich Koleshnya.[15]

2
BEFORE THE STORM

The overall deterioration of Sino-Soviet relations at the end of the 1950s was basically conditioned by ideological disagreements between the leadership of the CPSU and the Communist Party of China (CPC). The main issues for which the sides had opposing points of view were the assessment of Stalin's legacy, the possibility of peaceful coexistence of states with a different social order, problems of war and peace, the economic experiments in China, etc.

While Stalin was alive, with his indisputable authority, Chairman Mao did not even try to stand as an equal with him. With the exit of the Soviet leader, and as the PRC became stronger, however, Mao Zedong became proactive for the purpose of gaining a leading role in the world communist movement. Naturally, Moscow did not like this, and at that time an open polemic began.

Mao was extremely negative toward the debunking of Stalin's cult of personality, the beginning of which was marked by Khrushchev's famous speech at the XX Congress of the CPSU. The Chinese leader considered Stalin to be a real revolutionary, a true follower of Lenin; therefore, he perceived the critical remarks in the address by the Soviet leader as a departure from the principal positions of Marxism-Leninism. Some contemporary authors say, without substantiation, that Mao, in fact, hated Stalin and envied him. One cannot confirm or deny this statement; however, in his polemic against the Soviet leadership Mao said the following:

> Under the leadership of Stalin the Communist Party of the Soviet Union and the Soviet nation solidly and without deviation conducted in their country a line toward socialist industrialisation and collectivisation of agriculture, and achieved great success in the matter of socialist transformation and socialist competition.
>
> Under the leadership of Stalin the Communist Party of the Soviet Union, the Soviet nation, and the Soviet Army, fighting exceptionally hard battles, won a great victory in the anti-Fascist war.
>
> I.V. Stalin defended and developed Marxism-Leninism in the struggle against opportunists of all stripes, against the enemies of Leninism – the followers of Trotsky, Zinovyev, Bukharin, and other agents of the bourgeoisie.
>
> In his theoretical works, which are immortal works of Marxism-Leninism, I.V. Stalin made an unfading contribution to the matter of the international communist movement.

Speaking generally, under Stalin's leadership the Communist Party of the Soviet Union and the Soviet Government conducted a foreign policy that served proletarian internationalism and rendered enormous support to the revolutionary struggle of the nations of the world, including the revolutionary struggle of the Chinese people.

I.V. Stalin led the struggle, being at the very front edge of the historical stream; he was an implacable enemy of imperialism and all reactionaries.

All of Stalin's efforts were closely associated with the struggle of the great Communist Party of the Soviet Union and the great Soviet nation, and were inseparable from the revolutionary struggle of the nations of the entire world.

Stalin's life and efforts are the life and efforts of a great Marxist-Leninist, a great proletarian revolutionary.'[1]

Mao gave a derogatory and, for the most part, prophetic characterisation of the Soviet leaders who had taken the reins of government in the Soviet Union: 'Nationalists and careerists, Kremlin bribe-takers came to power in the USSR after 1953. When the time comes, they will throw down their masks, throw out their party cards, and openly govern their counties as feudal lords and serfs.'[2]

Another theme for which there was practically complete misunderstanding was the relationship to capitalist countries. Mao viewed a third world war as a boon, inasmuch as he had no doubts regarding the destruction of imperialism. The Chinese leader viewed the death of millions of people as the unavoidable cost of achieving the great goal: the victory of communism on a world scale. The Soviet leaders thought otherwise, inasmuch as many of them had fought in the Great Patriotic War and could well imagine the scale of misery in case of a repetition of something similar. Thus, the Kremlin was inclined toward peaceful coexistence with capitalism.

When in 1959 China provoked a border war with India, the Soviet leadership took a neutral position. This angered Mao, because the USSR was, in fact, demonstrating an unwillingness to help a communist power in its struggle against a capitalist power.

A subjective factor also played a role of no small importance in the rupture of relations: at times, Khrushchev allowed himself to address Mao with not enough respect, and the latter perceived any criticism as being extremely hurtful (and answered in kind). Mao probably considered himself to be the more distinguished revolutionary in comparison with Khrushchev and his entourage. Mao's contemptuous attitude toward Khrushchev sometimes broke through in a rather unexpected form. Here, for example, is how V.V. Ovchinnikov, *Pravda's* correspondent in the PRC, described the meeting between Khrushchev and Mao during the celebrations in honour of the 10th anniversary of the CPC:

After the festive celebrations Mao invited his Soviet guest to his residence near the capital. Confusion awaited Khrushchev there. His host met him in the swimming pool and suggested that [Khrushchev] join him. The problem, however, was that Nikita Sergeyevich could not swim. In black underpants that went down to his knees, he could only go into the water up to his waist and sit a few times to immerse himself, as he had done on a vacation in Pitsunda.

One can imagine how awkward the guest looked as compared with his host, who was able to easily swim across the kilometre-wide Yangtze! Khrushchev was so furious that he announced that evening that he was postponing the week-long trip across China that we had carefully prepared, and that he intended to return to the Motherland.

The reasons for the falling out between Peking and Moscow, which led to a 30-year confrontation and fighting on Damansky Island, were not only an ideological disagreement, but also the personal enmity between the two leaders. Recollections of the helpless figure in long underpants, when he was floundering in the swimming pool next to 'the great helmsman', strengthened this feeling for Khrushchev.[3]

A particular manifestation of the problems that had arisen was the exacerbation of the border issue. In his memoirs, Khrushchev wrote about how the Soviet leadership tried to resolve this problem:

One more stumbling block – the border problems. Now, in the light of our conflict with China, the question once again rises about the borders between the socialist countries. These problems have always existed. For the first time in Soviet history, however, an international conflict arose in the dispute with the People's Republic of China. We usually always managed to resolve this problem, making mutual concessions and adjusting the borderline. When at the beginning of the conflict with China we were looking for a resolution for the problem, we also thought about ceding to China some territory in exchange for some Chinese territory of equal value in areas that suited both sides. I was brought a list of claims the Chinese had brought forth. Malinovsky, Gromyko and I met. We thought that we had just

Mao Zedong and N. S. Khrushchev in 1958. They are still smiling at one another. (Military Museum of Hanoi, via Albert Grandolini)

resolved everything. I took a pencil and drew a line that divided the mutual claims on, as it were, a 50–50 basis. The border was more aligned.

We expected no particular complications, because the majority of these areas were not populated: neither our [people] nor Chinese lived there. Sometimes, perhaps, hunters and shepherds came by. In a word, a silly dispute. The Chinese, however, specifically wanted to create a conflict and refused to take part in the talks. They presented the USSR with absurd demands, declaring their 'right' to Vladivostok, Pamir, and other places. Now, five years later, we are meeting again. Deputy Minister of Foreign Affairs Vasily Kuznetsov went to Peking. Perhaps, after five more years, we will meet with the Chinese. The conflict is essentially not a question of borders, but of great international politics.[4]

Not only Mao and the Chinese communists were convinced that their country was being deprived of much territory for historical reasons. Well-known figure and democrat Sun Yatsen, the first president of the Republic of China, also viewed the expansive lands of neighbouring countries as Chinese and always dreamed of consolidating China into as large a size as possible.[5] Eternal enemy of the communists Chiang Kaishek even compiled a special list, noting in it territories that had been 'torn away' from the Chinese – Burma, the Amur River basin, Annam. This list included territories from which Chinese overlords had extracted tribute – Thailand, Nepal, Bhutan, Borneo, Java, Ceylon, etc.

Thus, Mao was not the first in his claims to neighbouring states. However, it was he who moved this problem to a practical plane.

Even earlier, PRC citizens had not observed the border regime very rigorously – they fished in Soviet waters, mowed grass on Soviet islands, etc. With mutual trust and good will, however, no one paid any attention to this. Here, for example, is how one of the history teachers from Heilongjiang University (Harbin) assessed the situation in a conversation with Soviet journalists:

In March 1858 a Russian official complained to China about a battalion armed to the teeth, about a convoy of vodka, moonshine, and a keg of port. A month later he returned to his home *krai* with a document confirming the right of the Russian Empire to thirty islands located along the Chinese bank of the Ussuri River…

Yes, of course, the border between the two powers 'did not run according to the rules', not along the middle of the river, but, for some reason, along the Chinese riverbank. The historical ties among the inhabitants of the two Ussuri riverbanks had, however, always been close. For example, the northern Chinese had always considered winter on ice normal, and in summer they made their way in boats to your territory and traded knick-knacks in the Russian villages for salt, bread, and eggs. Many even had some relatives in the USSR. The Soviet authorities turned a blind eye to this. However, when Stalin was removed from the Mausoleum and Mao Zedong declared Khrushchev to be an anathema, everything changed.[6]

7 February 1969. Chinese and Soviet border guards converse on the ice of the Ussuri River near the southern tip of Damansky. Directly under a target sign is I. Strelnikov. (Military Museum of Hanoi, via Albert Grandolini)

7 February 1969. Chinese and Soviet border guards converse on the ice of the Ussuri River near the southern tip of Damansky. I. Strelnikov is in the commander's hatch of the armoured personnel carrier. (Military Museum of Hanoi, via Albert Grandolini)

Border violators. (Military Museum of Hanoi, via Albert Grandolini)

Confrontation on the border. (Military Museum of Hanoi, via Albert Grandolini)

Starting in 1960, there were a large number of border violations. From hundreds to several thousands of incidents annually – this was the dynamic of the conflict that had developed.

In the mid-1960s the situation deteriorated in two respects. Firstly, local citizens loyal to the USSR began to be expelled to the hinterlands of the PRC. In their place arrived reserve servicemen of the People's Liberation Army of China (PLA). Secondly, border violations began to bear an intentional and blatantly challenging nature. As a rule, those who took part in these 'measures' carried signs calling on the Soviet border guards to reject 'revisionism' and rise under the banner of the ideas of Mao Zedong. There were also various calls to leave 'Chinese territory.'

Both PLA servicemen and persons in civilian clothing (who often were solders who had changed clothes) took part in similar actions. Border violations were rather often accompanied by cattle being driven off, land being ploughed up, and simply attempts to seize individual sectors of Soviet territory. To stop the provocations, Soviet border guards received an order to force the violators out from the territory of the USSR without using weapons, which was rigorously carried out.

The Chinese provoked the border guards several times into using weapons or brute force in order to film everything and then use it for propaganda purposes. However, they did not obtain any interesting shots from this point of view. For example, Chinese documentaries about events on the border presented scenes such as the expulsion of PRC citizens from Soviet territory with the help of long poles, the use of hoses against Chinese fishermen, etc. None of these scenes, however, in any way reached the level that required the use of strong terms such as 'crime,' 'cruelty,' 'atrocity,' etc. Rather the opposite: any unbiased observer could easily see some petty and persistent hooliganism in the actions of the Chinese themselves.

Vitialy Dmitriyevich Bubenin, who in 1969 was chief of the outpost, recalls the following:

> In the summer the Chinese usually attempted to set up their fishing nets near our riverbank. Despite the conditions of the Treaty of Tianjin, we did not object to the Chinese fishing in the river or their moving along the main channel on their boats. Closer to the mid-1960s, however, they began to behave differently. They began to accuse us of going 'along the wrong path'. They began to call us invaders and revisionists, and to use other political tidbits ... They, of course, blamed us, the border guards, for all their troubles.
>
> When the Chinese stopped being friendly, we began to expel them from Soviet territory. As soon as they set out on their boats to place their nets near our riverbank, an armoured border boat would appear and drive them away. The nets turned into shreds, and the Chinese had to quickly make a run for it.
>
> The Chinese also had boats that they used for provocations. They set up a sharpened piece of rail on the bow, like the Ancient Greek battering rams, accelerated, and tried to strike the side of our vessel.
>
> In the winter the Chinese acted differently. When the Ussuri froze, they began to come onto the ice in crowds.[7]

One time a *Pravda* correspondent visited Bubenin's outpost in the Kulebyakiny Hills. Bubenin told him the following:

Soviet border guards are ready to meet uninvited 'guests.' (Chinese Internet)

In front of the APC (from left to right): Colonel D.V. Leonov, Senior Lieutenants V.D. Bubenin (Chief of the 1st Border Outpost (Kulebyakiny Hills) of the Ussuri Border Detachment, which was adjacent to the right flank of the Nizhne-Mikhaylovka Outpost), I.I. Strelnikov, and V.N. Shorokhov (Chief of the 3rd Border Outpost (Lastochka) of the Ussuri Border Detachment, which was adjacent to the left flank of the Nizhne-Mikhaylovka Outpost). (Military Museum of Hanoi, via Albert Grandolini)

> The situation was thus – a fisherman came, stuck a portrait of Mao on a pole in the snow, and began to hammer away at a hole. We explained to him: you cannot violate the border. We led him away. The next day 20 fishermen arrived. Three nets, but each one had a quotation book. They waved them in order to fish better. We led them away. They brought about 500 people to the border. Women and children; they held a rally, beat drums. They were loaded on vehicles – to the Soviet riverbank. Our guys stood in a chain. The vehicles headed toward them, counting on scaring them. It didn't happen – they left. They came with banners: quotations were hooked on clubs, iron pipes on top of poles. Our guys once again were a wall. They put their quotations in their pockets, the clubs swinging. Nothing – they were driven away.[8]

Nevertheless, the number of border violations increased, and this forced the Soviet authorities to adopt some additional measures.

On 30 April 1965, the USSR Council of Ministers adopted a resolution, 'On Strengthening the Security of the State Border of the USSR on Sectors of the Eastern, Far Eastern, and Pacific Ocean Border Districts.' In accordance with this resolution, the number of border guards was substantially increased, and their provision with combat and engineer equipment was improved.

On 4 February 1967, a new resolution from the CC CPSU and USSR Council of Ministers was passed: 'On Strengthening the State Border between the USSR and People's Republic of China.' It envisioned the establishment of the Transbaikal Border District, several new border detachments, outposts, and manoeuvre groups, and an increase in the number of border guards.

Contemporary Chinese sources confirm the fact of the numerous conflicts on the border at that time, although they lay the blame for what happened mainly on the Soviets. Yes, they say, Soviet border guards did not, in fact, use weapons, but the clashes sometimes resulted in victims on the Chinese side. As an example, they cite events in winter 1967-1968 on Kirkinsky (Qiliqin) Island. At that time armoured transports were used to drive the Chinese out, which, according to Chinese information, resulted in the death of four PRC citizens.

Possibly it is specifically this event to which Colonel (retired) Grigory Andreyevich Skladanyuk is referring in the following. At that time he was a major and chief of the Sergeants School:

> In 1965 we, the border guards, began to sharply feel the changes that were happening in relations between the USSR and China. In the context of their presentation of territorial claims to the USSR, the Chinese began to wilfully occupy our islands on the Ussuri River.
>
> I want to talk about one episode with which few people, except for those who directly took part in it, are familiar. Nothing about this was printed or spoken about on the radio. It happened in December 1967. More than 1,000 Chinese attempted to blatantly

cross the border on a sector of the Kulebyakiny Hills Border Outpost of the Iman Border Detachment.

At night, the Chinese gouged out the ice on the Ussuri River in order to hinder our border squads from moving along the borderline. I was ordered by Chief of the Border Detachment Colonel Demokrat Vladimirovich Leonov to pick out a group of cadets from the sergeants school and go there and fill up the ice holes.

We were already finishing up the work, when we saw that a crowd was moving from the Chinese riverbank; they were in motor vehicles, on tractors, and in carts.

The crowd was aggressive, shouting and roaring. In addition to anti-Soviet slogans, the Chinese were carrying clubs, crowbars, shovels, and harpoons. Nails had been driven into the wooden part of the harpoons and clubs, which were covered by quotations or portraits of Mao. When I reported the situation to Colonel Leonov, I received an order from him: do not permit border violations from the adjacent territory. I had several dozen border guards and two BTR-60PB armoured personnel carriers at my disposal; the Chinese had an angry crowd much larger than us. We made a chain of ourselves along the borderline. We were not using weapons. The Chinese *en masse* rushed at our chain, and, several people thick, attempted to encircle our border guards and capture us. By the way, at this time cadet Yu. V. Babansky (future Hero of the Soviet Union for the fighting on 2 March 1969) had been torn away from the common chain. I had to order the armoured personnel carrier driver to force back the invading crowd with the help of the equipment so as to prevent a breach into

Kirkinsky Island, 13 December 1967. On the extreme left is V.D. Bubenin. (Military Museum of Hanoi, via Albert Grandolini)

Damansky Island. 22 January 1969. Soviet border guards drive out the Chinese from Soviet territory. (Military Museum of Hanoi, via Albert Grandolini)

The border boat *Steregushchy* tries to force a Chinese fisherman from Soviet waters. (Chinese Internet)

our territory and not allow the Chinese to encircle our border guards and take them prisoner. We carried out the task and prohibited border violations. We suffered no losses as a result of this clash, although many border guards were injured. Several Chinese fell under the wheels of the armoured personnel carriers (the Chinese later informed us that five had died).

The Chinese had prepared this provocation earlier. This is attested by the fact that dozens of correspondents, including foreign ones, appeared literally instantly from Chinese territory. The correspondents had begun to document on tape everything that was happening. When the crowd left for the Chinese riverbank, loudspeakers from the PRC were turned on, through which the Chinese shouted in Russian insults at us and threats of cracking down on our border guards.[9]

Chinese violate the border and shout slogans; a Soviet officer smokes, barely restraining his emotions. (Military Museum of Hanoi, via Albert Grandolini)

As is obvious, Skladanyuk's recollections and the Chinese materials do not concur regarding the number of PRC citizens who died. However, this situation is characteristic for the history of the events with China.

Here is how V.D. Bubenin described one of the altercations of February 1968:

A sharp command sounded from the amplifier. The entire crowd numbering several hundred turned in our direction. I was scared. On the faces of the Chinese were grimaces of evil and hatred. They were all hysterically yelling, shaking their fists, slogans, and posters, already having let fly cartons with inscriptions, and clubs with those nails could be seen…

The furious crowd, having been brought to a state of the effects of skilled psychological treatment and reinforced with alcohol, was at the very next instant already rushing at us. As many as ten movie cameras, which had been set up on the other riverbank, were taking pictures. A large number of officials in paramilitary and military uniforms were crowding around there too. They were all ready for a decisive battle.

And so it began. Thousands of select, healthy, strong, and angry soldiers grappled in mortal combat. Powerful wild roars, groans, shouts, and screams for help resounded far above the great Ussuri River. The cracking of stakes and rifle butts, skulls and bones supplemented the picture of the battle.[10]

Unfortunately, it is very difficult to find truthful recollections of Chinese participants in these events. What has been published in China often bears a purely propagandistic character, while articles in Western sources present, as a rule, a mixture of truth and myth. For example, in the February (1997) issue of the journal *Kempo*, a certain Hui Mizhou from Montreal published recollections from his army commander. Supposedly he himself served in the PLA Special Forces, and his immediate chief was one Jian Zhou, an officer-instructor from the special unit of the 49th Field Army.

Upon an attentive reading of the article, one can detect the presence of both truthful and unreliable information (also anecdotal). The following can be cited from the more reasonable content:

At first, everything boiled down to talking, but later words began to turn into fierce confrontation. The majority of skirmishes where force was used ended in favor [*sic*] of the bigger and stronger Soviet soldiers, who 'beat back' their Chinese opponents to 'that side of the border'. Chinese attempts to photograph these assaults (for the purpose of later using them for propaganda purposes) were neutralised by the Soviets, because the Soviet soldiers felt no shame in beating up the so-called 'journalists' and confiscating their film.

However, being loyal to their 'god' – Chairman Mao – and his revolutionary path, the Chinese soldiers returned over and over to Zhenbao Island to once again be beaten or even killed for their great leader. This increasingly irritated the Soviet servicemen, but the scuffles never escalated to the level of hand-to-hand clashes, since both sides feared the consequences of using weapons. Therefore, these skirmishes became known as 'group scuffles'.[11]

As mentioned above, the Soviets adopted specific preventive measures; however, in several cases instructions 'from above' were very vague. Here is an eloquent example of this. In summer 1968 a meeting was held in Khabarovsk, chaired by USSR Deputy Minister of Foreign Affairs Vasily Vasilyevich Kuznetsov. Among those who attended the meeting were, in particular, Colonel Demokrat Vladimirovich Leonov (chief of the Iman Border Detachment) and Lieutenant Colonel Aleksandr Dmitriyevich Konstantinov (chief of the political section of the detachment).

The border guards expected to hear clear and unambiguous directives regarding border violations, but General Colonel P.I. Zyryanov limited himself to perfunctory observations: 'Do not allow the Chinese onto Soviet territory, do not use weapons.' This old and bad habit among some Soviet commanders – try to not take

Colonel Demokrat Vladimirovich Leonov, chief of the Iman Border Detachment. (photo© The Khabarovsk Territorial Museum after N.I. Grodekov)

responsibility upon oneself – would have an impact later in the heat of battle on Damansky. In the meantime, there was already fighting going on with poles, chains, rifle butts, and automatic weapons. The question as to whether or not under these conditions there would soon be fighting using guns was a rhetorical one.

Envisioning the worst-case scenario for the development of events, the Iman Border Detachment command wrote to the command of the border district for clarification. The officers expressed themselves imprudently to the Military Council; they said that they were receiving no guidance from them.[12]

The district command latched on to this sentence and arranged a good dressing down for the signatories. The sole positive result of this was an instruction for the district commander: if the Chinese opened fire, this was to be answered with the same. However, this was already clear; otherwise, why, in general, were border guards needed at that time?

Information about a possible conflict came not only from the border guards, but also from the KGB. The latter's work in China was extremely difficult, inasmuch as after the PRC was formed the Soviet leadership had done the unthinkable – it betrayed its in-country agents to the Chinese. Some historians think that by this act Stalin wanted to demonstrate to the Chinese leadership his sincerity, honesty, and special trust.[13] It has been suggested that the Soviet leader had considered the possibility of disclosing the agent network after the CPC came to power, and, therefore, was simply pre-empting the event. Obviously, only specialists can evaluate the validity of such a suggestion.

Stalin's decision probably resulted in the death of people who trusted Soviet intelligence, and, moreover, deprived Moscow of truthful information about what was happening in China. Even under these conditions, however, Soviet agents were able to find answers to many questions. Former station chief in Peking Yuri Ivanovich Drozdov describes one of the episodes of his work as follows:

> I managed to be in the province of Heilongjiang, in Harbin, and met with our elderly countrymen. One of them said that the Chinese authorities had evicted him from the apiary that belonged to him, and turned it into a huge sandbox, which are in the tactics classes at the military academies. The terrain represented on it was the image of a sector of adjacent Soviet territory. The 84-year-old Cossack officer was very puzzled.
>
> In a conversion with me, a representative from the Krupp Firm in Peking called the Russians fools for not seeing what was going on under their noses. He expressed concern, inasmuch as he had been where the Soviets were not allowed. Krupp is steel, and steel is needed for war. My Western colleagues, who were observing Sino-Soviet border relations, carefully made it known that the Chinese were strengthening the military grouping on the border with the USSR.
>
> We consolidated this and other information and sent reports to the Centre, requesting that the information be verified by space and radio-technical resources, and military and border intelligence. No answer followed. In fall 1967 I flew to the Centre on leave, where my direct boss announced that my encryptions would cause him another heart attack. I was silent. In our subunit they told me that the alarming cipher was sent to the higher authorities, from where it was returned with a threatening reply: "Verify this. If this is not confirmed, punish the station chief." They verified it and everything was confirmed. There were no apologies. This was not done.
>
> In 1969, in the area near the apiary, the well-known armed conflict took place.[14]

On Damansky the situation deteriorated each day. The time had passed when contact between the Chinese and the Soviet border guards were relatively peaceful; now, in accordance with the inexorable logic of events, this transformed into massive brawls. Even before the beginning of the fighting, several dozen border guards received government awards, and someone was retired from the army on disability.

Extremely fierce fighting took place on 22 January 1969. The following was written about this day in a report to the command:

> On 22 January 1969 at 11.15hrs, 25 armed Chinese servicemen began to walk around Damansky Island. Upon a demand for them to leave our territory, the Chinese began to shout quotations from Mao and wave their fists. Flouting standards of behaviour on the border, the Chinese servicemen shouted slogans and, waving weapons (machine guns and carbines), they rushed at our border guards. Senior Lieutenant Strelnikov ordered that the men protect themselves against Chinese blows, using rifle butts. The chief of the Chinese post ordered his soldiers to incapacitate Senior Lieutenant Strelnikov. Private A.G. Denisenko protected the officer, despite the fact that he himself had received a blow across his face from a rifle butt; he saved his commander from certain death.[15]

As a result of this fight, the Soviet border guards captured several machine guns and carbines from their Chinese 'colleagues'.[16] Upon subsequent examination of the weapons it became clear that the cartridges had already been chambered, that is, they were ready to be used quickly. Thus, any random shot at that time could have resulted in an armed conflict. The Chinese began to openly threaten Strelnikov: 'Black Ivan, we will kill you.'

A brawl on Damansky, 22 January 1969. On the left, waving a pistol in a holster, is Chief of the Hunzy Border Post Sun Yuguo. (Military Museum of Hanoi, via Albert Grandolini)

Chinese weapons captured by Soviet border guards in the hand-to-hand fighting against the provocateurs on 22 January 1969. (Military Museum of Hanoi, via Albert Grandolini)

The Soviet commanders clearly understood how unfavourably the situation was developing, and, therefore, they were always calling for special vigilance from their subordinates. Some measures were adopted: for example, the staff of each border outpost was increased by as many as 50 men, and armoured personnel carriers (APC) were attached.

Nor did the chiefs of the outposts sit idly by, as hardly a day went by without some encounter with the Chinese; like no others, they sensed the approach of terrible events.

Several months before the war, the border guards of the second outpost (Nizhne-Mikhaylovka) of the Iman Border Detachment built shelters for their personnel, laid telephone cable to Damansky Island, outfitted observation posts, and cut through a clearing in the direction of the first border outpost (Kulebyakiny Hills).

The detachment command used the Nizhne-Mikhaylovka outpost several times to conduct officer classes. As for personnel manning and supplies of combat equipment, everything here was completely satisfactory.

The political department of the Iman Border Detachment (Lieutenant Colonel A.D. Konstantinov) took into account the features of the territory on this section of the border – challenging climatic conditions, remoteness from cultural centres, etc. Therefore, it tried in every way possible to ease the service that was already difficult even without these problems. For example, through the efforts of the political workers at the outposts, concerts by different creative teams were constantly being organised and meetings between the border guards and the local inhabitants were held.

On the 23 February 1969 holiday (Soviet Army and Navy Day), a group of Chinese border guards came out onto the ice of the Ussuri River and, quickly going to the southern extreme of Damansky, returned to their territory in formation and with a loud song. This action had no impression whatsoever on the border guards, who had gotten used to the provocations, and the concert of amateur performances and evening of dancing made them generally forget the unremarkable incident. No one could imagine that this would be the last holiday for 22 border guards of the second outpost.

3
AMBUSH

The Soviet people found out about the events of 2 March 1969 from a brief TASS report:

> Provocation of Chinese Authorities on the Soviet-Chinese Border
>
> On 2 March at 04.10hrs Moscow time, the Chinese authorities organised an armed provocation in the region of the Nizhne-Mikhaylovka border post (Damansky Island) on the Ussuri River. The armed Chinese detachment crossed the Soviet state border and made its way to Damansky Island.
>
> According to the Soviet border guards patrolling this area, the Chinese suddenly opened fire. There are dead and wounded.
>
> The decisive actions of the Soviet border guards drove the border violators out of Soviet territory.
>
> On 2 March 1969 the Soviet government sent the PRC government a note resolutely protesting the provocative actions of the Chinese authorities on the Sino-Soviet border. In particular, the note pointed out those provocative actions of the Chinese authorities on the Sino-Soviet border would be rebuffed and decisively stopped.[1]

The above-mentioned note mentioned several details:[2] the estimated number of border violators, the ambush organised by the Chinese, and the participation of several groups of provocateurs in the fighting. Ritual phrases were cited here about the responsibility of the Chinese and the feelings of friendship for the Chinese people. It is significant that, lodging a protest, the USSR leadership at the same time demanded that this matter be investigated and the guilty punished – as if Mao and his entourage were themselves not the organisers of the provocation.

However, neither the note nor the TASS report gave a clear picture of the events that had taken place. Strictly speaking, even the Kremlin was not aware of all the details. Only gradually did the picture of the armed clash emerge. The events developed as follows.

On the night of 1-2 March 1969, around 300 PLA servicemen crossed over to Damansky Island and lay down among the bushes and trees on the higher western bank of the island (see Sketch Map 1). They did not dig trenches, but simply lay in the snow, first putting down mats.

The estimated number of Chinese was determined after the battle, according to the number of foxholes: as a rule, 306 were cited. A 1992 Chinese book states that the following subunits arrived on Damansky:

- an intelligence company from 133rd Division (a total of two platoons);
- an intelligence platoon from 133rd Division's 397th Regiment;
- 1st platoon of the 1st Company of 73rd Division's 217th Regiment.

The following PLA officers commanded these subunits:

- Ma Xianjie – Chief of 133rd Division's intelligence department;
- Cao Jianhua – Deputy Chief of Staff of one of the military subdistricts;
- Chen Shaoguang – Deputy Commander of 133rd Division's intelligence company;
- Wang Qingrong – Deputy Commander of 217th Regiment's 1st company.[3]

The latter two died in the battle that unfolded; as for the first two, Chinese sources report nothing about their subsequent fate.

The Chinese soldiers' gear was completely appropriate for the weather conditions and consisted of the following:

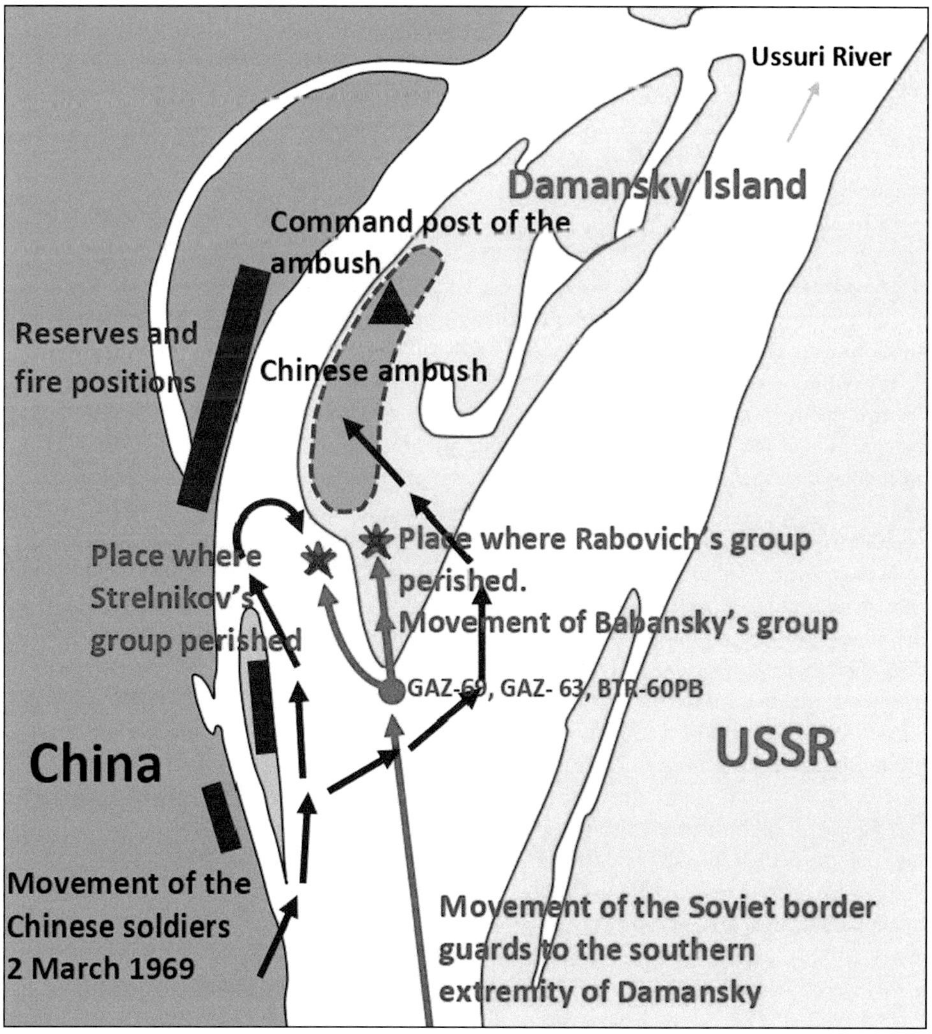

Sketch Map 1: Beginning of the battle on 2 March 1969. (authors' drawing)

- hats with earflaps [*ushanka*], which differed from the similar Soviet *ushanka* in that the former had two flaps on the left and right to better pick up sounds. Soldiers in the Japanese Kwantung Army had such flaps on their winter headgear; it is possible that the Chinese copied this. The Chinese *ushanka* was decorated with a red plastic star, very much like the Soviet star;
- insulated jackets and pants;
- laced shoes, resembling insulated sneakers;
- warm underwear;
- thick socks;
- army-style mittens – large, with the index finger separate and the other fingers together.

From right to left: Private Vladimir Koyakhov, Junior Lieutenant Mikhail Koleshnya and Private Mikhail Akhmetgareyev on the bank of the Ussuri River, March 1969. (photo© The Khabarovsk Territorial Museum after N.I. Grodekov)

The Chinese were armed with Kalashnikov assault rifles (AK-47) and Simonov self-loading carbines (SKS-45). They also had Degtyarev light machine guns (RPD) and light antitank grenade launchers (RPG-2). The commanders had TT (Tulsky Tokarev) pistols. Almost all Chinese weapons had been produced on Soviet models. The cartridge magazines for the AKs and cartridge clips for the SKSs were stored in chest pouches.

The Chinese soldiers wore white camouflage smocks (more correctly, capes held by a knot at the neck). They carried no documents in their pockets.

The Chinese installed a telephone line on the Chinese riverbank and lay in the snow until morning, warming them up with 'hanja' (rice vodka) and snacking on biscuits. The vodka was rationed at 100 grams per man, with the condition that it be used in small swallows over a long period of time (the advice of military doctors).

It is still not known precisely at what time the Chinese arrived on the island, because Chinese sources are very vague in their specification of this time – 'around midnight' or 'after midnight.' The air temperature that night had dropped to, minus 27 degrees celsius[4] and, as Chinese publications state, this was the reason for several cases of frostbite.

To support the subunits landing on Damansky Island, recoilless rifle, medium machine gun, and mortar positions were outfitted on the Chinese riverbank. Several hundred infantrymen were biding their time there.[5]

On the night of 2 March, two border guards were continuously located at the Soviet observation post (Mount Kafyla), but they did not notice or hear anything – no fire, no sounds. The distance of the post from the island (more than three kilometres), the snow that was falling all night, and the limited visibility through the optical instruments of that time all played a role here. The Chinese ambush might have been detected from the air, but border aviation did not fly on Sunday. It is possible that the Chinese chose 2 March for the attack for two other reasons. Firstly, considerable border guard forces were involved in joint exercises with the troops of the Far Eastern Military District, and, therefore, could not immediately take part in the battle. Secondly, it was at this time that in Russia it was customary to celebrate Shrovetide[6], that is to bid farewell to winter. The organisers of the provocation could have been relying on the hospitality of the local Soviet authorities, for whom an invitation to dinner that day for the chief of the border guards seemed to be a completely natural matter. Thus, the advance of the Chinese was well thought out and was organised in absolute secrecy.

Border guards Private Aleksandr Shevtsov and Private Vladimir Koyakhov were at the observation post on the morning of 2 March. At around 10.40 Soviet local time, they noticed the advance of a group of armed men (numbering as many as 30 men) from the Hunzy (Chinese) Border Post in the direction of Damansky. Meanwhile, at first the Chinese had held a small rally, accompanied by the waving of Mao's quotation books; then they set off for the island. Private Shevtsov, who was the senior man of the border detail, immediately reported this by telephone to the Nizhne-Mikhaylovka Outpost, which was located six kilometres southeast of the island.

Senior Lieutenant Ivan Strelnikov, chief of the outpost, called his subordinates 'to arms' after which he called the border detachment's duty officer and his neighbour, Vitaly Bubenin.

Valery Pavlovich Fateyev, former Sergeant Major of the Nizhne-Mikhaylovka Outpost, recalls:

> It was Sunday. Everything was as usual. I remember the weather was good. I had been given the task of taking some men and … dragging ice into coolers. Since at that time there were no electric refrigerators, we were digging a cooler pit in the ground. We had just reached the river and started working, when the outpost sentry called out "Outpost, to arms!" As the Sergeant Major of the outpost, my task was to hand out the new sheepskin coats … In case of Chinese provocations, we had new coats and felt boots for actions to stop them. The border guards had to stand for a very long time. And it was cold … An outpost was built. The chief of the outpost came out. I reported that the outpost had been built.[7]

Personnel loaded up in three vehicles – the commander's GAZ-69 (Strelnikov himself and six or seven other men), a BTR-60PB APC (around 13 men, the senior man was Sergeant V. Rabovich), and a GAZ-63 (total of 12 border guards, headed by Junior Sergeant

Private Aleksandr Shevtsov. It was he who reported to the outpost about the movement of the group of provocateurs to Damansky on the morning of 2 March 1969. (photo© The Khabarovsk Territorial Museum after N.I. Grodekov)

The first photo shows PLA soldiers (at a distance of around 300 metres). Because of the distance, it is difficult to precisely make out the number of men: somewhere between 22 and 24. (Some veterans say that the first photo was taken not on 2 March, but rather earlier, inasmuch as the Chinese here are standing on their riverbank, while on 2 March they had deployed in a chain between Damansky and the Chinese riverbank.)

The second photo shows about 10 Chinese and three border guards (assumed to be I. Strelnikov, N. Buinevich, and A. Denisenko) coming to meet them. It is completely obvious that Damansky is on the right: somewhere here, among the bare trees and shrubbery, the Chinese ambush silently waited.

We will never know if at the last moment Strelnikov's suspicions arose that this time the meeting with the Chinese would not end as it usually did. He was a very experienced commander and, therefore, might have noticed their strange behaviour. usually they waved quotation books and loudly shouted and cursed, but this morning they were silent and seemed to be tensely waiting for something.

According to Soviet information, at around 11.15hrs Strelnikov came practically right up to the Chinese. A document compiled by the PLA General Staff for the higher-level CPC party functionaries indicated the time more precisely: 9.17hrs.[9] It more likely was this, because in organising the attack the Chinese probably kept track of the time and continuously took photographs of and filmed the events.

One can judge the following subsequent brief dialogue with a good degree of certainty. The fact is that a meeting of the border guards of the two neighbouring sides was always accompanied by a certain ritual, inasmuch as at this time they were authorised representatives of their countries. This means that Strelnikov probably protested the border violation and demanded that the Chinese servicemen leave USSR territory.

One of the Chinese answered loudly.

Inasmuch as in any army there exists strict discipline, and in this respect the PLA was distinguished by particular strictness, one can assume that this Chinese was the commander of the group. As Soviet witnesses say, on this day the commander was Sun Yuguo, Chief of the Hunzy Border Post. Chinese materials indirectly attest that he answered in the sense that this land belonged to China (by the way, some Chinese authors say that another man – detachment Commander Wu Yonggao, who was there – had answered Strelnikov). Following this, two pistol shots were heard: they came from staff officer Jin Qinlong, who was located in the ambush. This gave the general signal for the commencement of the operation.

Yu. Babansky). There were two officers: Strelnikov and Senior Lieutenant N. Buinevich, the special operations officer.[8]

The GAZ-63 was an auto repair vehicle with a rather weak engine; therefore, on the way to the island, it lagged behind the main group by around 15 minutes. It was just this unforeseen delay that saved the lives of Babansky and several soldiers: had they arrived at Damansky with everyone else, they would not have been living witnesses to the commencement of the fighting.

At this time the Chinese divided up: one group (around 12 men) moved on the ice of the Ussuri and stopped between the island and the Chinese riverbank at a distance of around 300 metres from the southern end of Damansky. The remaining Chinese (around 18 men) rounded the southern end of the island and then set off for the ambush. It seems that in this way they were trying to imply to the Soviet border guards that the route was across the island, from east to west, directly into the ambush.

Having arrived at the place, the command GAZ and APC stopped at the southern end of Damansky. Having hurried there, the border guards moved in two groups in the direction of the Chinese: the chief himself led the first group (seven men) along the ice, while Rabovich's group went in parallel directly around the island.

Here it should be mentioned that the movement of both groups took place without preparatory reconnaissance of the terrain, which resulted in the death of the majority of the border guards. The chief of the outpost cannot, however, be blamed for this: such practice was standard and was never questioned. It is another matter that the Soviet commanders had not seen that moment when the Chinese had begun their preparation to conduct a large-scale provocation. In this respect, a large part of the blame lies on intelligence.

Private Nikolay Petrov, a photographer who filmed what took place with a movie camera and with a Zorky-4 camera, rode with Strelnikov. Petrov's last three pictures attest that events unfolded in just this way, and not otherwise.

Third of Private N. Petrov's photos. (Military Museum of Hanoi, via Albert Grandolini)

Thus, the shooting of the group of border guards could have taken place differently. A book by Chinese authors Sun Xiao and Zuo Dun states that the first shot was fired by a certain Zhou Dengguo, who allegedly pre-empted Strelnikov, who was trying to use his own pistol.[10] Then, they say, other Chinese soldiers also began to fire. If we discard the fabrications about the pistol in this description, then it could have been this way: the order to open fire against the border guards had clearly been given earlier to certain soldiers – to this very Zhou Dengguo and others. How they were positioned here is not known.

What happened immediately after this is well known: the Chinese immediately shot Strelnikov and his group. But how this happened is not completely understood.

The majority of researchers and border guard veterans think that immediately before the firing the Chinese stood before Strelnikov in two rows. Allegedly, after the signal to attack, the first row suddenly separated and the second group opened surprise automatic fire. Petrov's third photograph is cited as proof: it shows the separating Chinese and the closest PLA soldier raising his arm – as a signal to open fire.

In principle, this all could have been so; therefore, this version should not be tossed out. However, there are some doubts. Firstly, in the photograph it is obvious that the Chinese are moving chaotically, and there is no second row behind them. Moreover, all those in the picture have weapons behind their backs. Secondly, the raised hand of one of the Chinese could signal that either he did not want to be caught in the picture or he simply was covering his face from the sun. Pay attention to the orientation of the shadows of the Chinese on the ice: the sun is shining in the face of the one who raised his arm.

Strelnikov's group and the chief of the outpost himself died immediately. The Chinese, who had run up to them, took Petrov's motion picture camera from his hands, but they did not notice the camera for taking still photographs: the Soviet soldier had fallen on it, covering it with his sheepskin coat.

The ambush on Damansky also opened fire – against Rabovich's group. At the same time, the machine guns, mortars, and recoilless rifles on the Chinese riverbank could be heard: the sounds of shots fused into a single, uninterrupted roar.

Rabovich managed to shout 'To battle!' after which the soldiers, walking one behind the other, dispersed in a chain in the direction of the ambush. However, this still did not resolve anything: some of the Soviet border guards were killed or wounded, and those who were still alive were in plain sight of the Chinese.

Some of the attackers stood up from their 'foxholes' and rushed to attack the handful of Soviet soldiers. The latter accepted battle and literally fought to their last bullet.

When the bullets ran out, Corporal Davydenko grabbed a machine gun by the barrel and engaged in hand-to-hand fighting

Arrival of Babansky's group at the place of battle on 2 March 1969. The dark running figure at the left edge of the photo is Yu. Babansky. Driver P. Kovalev is standing on the roof of the APC: he is shouting for the border guards to rush to the aid of I. Strelnikov. (Chinese Internet)

with the Chinese surrounding him – and this when he was already seriously wounded. Other border guards behaved just as bravely.

Yu. Babansky's group arrived literally a few minutes before the beginning of the firing.

Private Vladimir Razmakhnin was also in this group. He describes the commencement of the battle in March 1969 as follows:

> Since the truck moved more slowly than the APC and GAZ-69, my group arrived at the island later. An APC was standing near it, and the driver said that we should quickly follow on the island to Senior Lieutenant Strelnikov. None of our weapons were loaded. While we were running we saw that the group of border guards from our outpost was standing with the chief opposite the group of provocateurs and gesticulating, apparently demanding that they leave our territory. One provocateur was standing somewhat to the side, with a weapon in his hands. I had run up to around 100 metres – maybe more – from the outpost chief's group, when I saw that the provocateur who had been standing to the side had reloaded the shutter and opened fire at the island and in our direction. I could not see the outpost chief's entire group or what had happened there. I also did not see, but the firing also continued there.[11]

Having taken up a position at some distance behind his dead comrades, Babansky and other border guards met the attacking Chinese with machine gun fire. They did not have many bullets – each had two incomplete magazines (25 bullets in each); there were no grenades at all.

The attackers reached the positions of Rabovich's group, and here they finished off the wounded border guards at point-blank range, with rifle butts and cold steel – bayonets and knives. This fact, which will forever be disgraceful for the PLA, is attested by documents from the Soviet medical commission and photographs by military correspondent Vladimir Grechukhin.

Private Gennady Serebrov was the only one who, literally miraculously, remained alive. Regaining consciousness in a hospital, he reported about the last minutes of the life of his friends:

> We tried to move so as to continuously keep the group headed by the chief of the outpost in our field of vision. Private Yegupov was walking in front of me. Suddenly, I saw Chinese lying on the snow behind the trees. They were aiming their rifles at us. Then we heard a loud shout, apparently the order to open fire. Bullets struck Yegupov, and he fell on the snow. I immediately shot a long burst from the machine gun at the Chinese. They stood from their hiding places and came directly toward us, firing on the move. I attempted to take cover behind a tree, but felt a strong blow to my leg, above the knee, then a second, a third, and a feeling as if it was being torn to pieces, and then I lost consciousness.[12]

Why, however did Rabovich's group, having seen the overwhelming numerical superiority of the enemy, not withdraw? There are several possible explanations for this. First and foremost, it is not known precisely how many border guards survived after the first Chinese salvo: it is possible that there was no one left to withdraw. In addition, there was no sense in withdrawing, inasmuch as the Soviet soldiers were in a completely open area, in the immediate vicinity of the attacking Chinese. Finally, a particular psychological state of mind of the border guards – Not a single step back! – could have played a role. Several veterans of these events speak about this trait.

Meanwhile, Babansky and his subordinates continued in the unequal fighting. Initially they fired long bursts – because of the unexpectedness of what was happening and hatred of the enemy. Fewer and fewer soldiers remained in the group, and the ammunition was quickly being used up. When it became quite desperate with the cartridges, Banbansky and those who remained in formation tried to take them from the dead, but the latter had almost none left. Babansky sent Private Yeremin to the telephone outlet, which was located on the riverbank. Yeremin was wounded but reached the outlet.

Yury Kozus, Vladimir Yerukh, Anatoly Rekut, Vladimir Yezhov, Vasily Vishnevsky, Abzaldin Bikuzin, and Vladimir Razmakhnin were firing next to Babansky. Fewer and fewer forces remained. Having assessed the situation, the junior sergeant made the decision to withdraw to where the vehicles were parked; however, at the moment Chinese artillery was covering the GAZ-69 and repair car.

The drivers of the vehicles had taken shelter in the APC that Strelnikov had left and had withdrawn beyond the island. It was then that Vitaly Bubenin and his soldiers arrived.

Yu. Babansky (on the right) and Yu. Kozus (on the left). (photo© The Khabarovsk Territorial Museum after N.I. Grodekov)

The GAZ-69 and GAZ-63 burn. On the right, Bubenin's APC and Strelnikov's APC can be seen. (Chinese Internet)

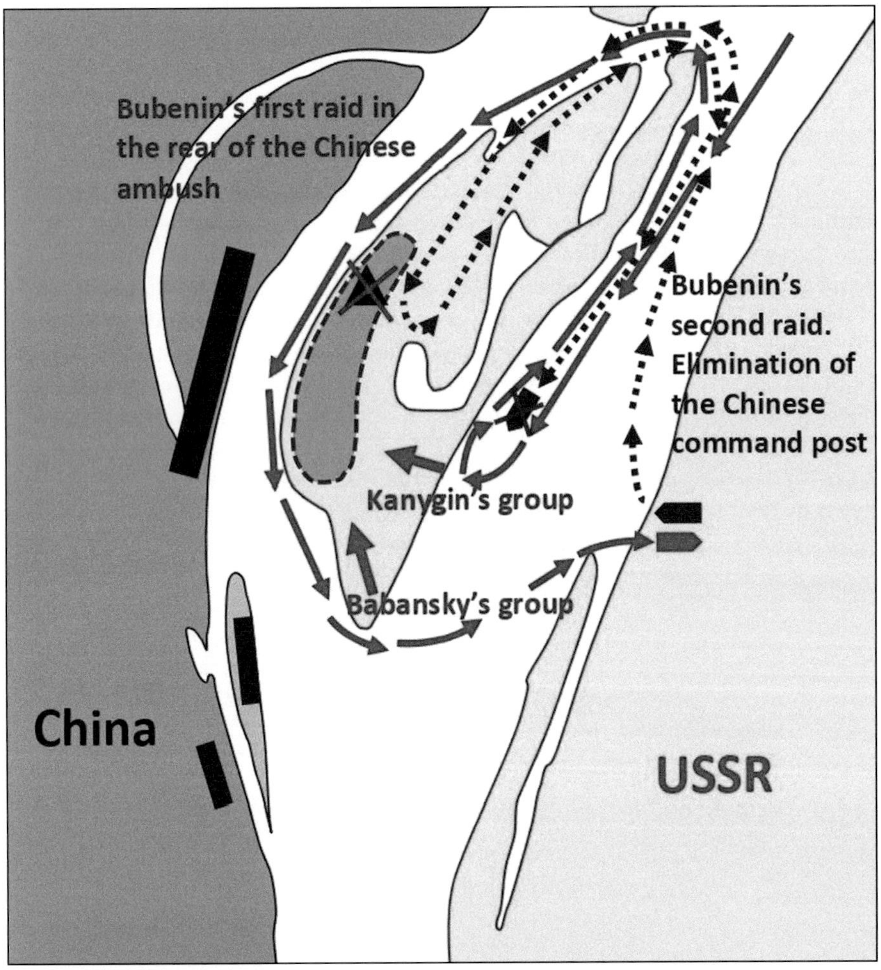

Sketch Map 2: End of the battle on 2 March 1969. (authors' drawing)

Senior Lieutenant Bubenin commanded the neighbouring Kulebyakiny Hills Outpost, which was located 17-18 kilometres north of Damansky. Having received a report on the morning of 2 March about what was happening on the island, he loaded his APC with 21 border guards and sped off to rescue his neighbours (thus, there were 23 men in Bubenin's APC: the 21 border guards, plus the driver-mechanic and Bubenin himself).

At around 11.30hrs the APC reached Damansky and continued to move along its eastern bank (see Sketch Map 2). Upon hearing heavy firing, the border guards dismounted from the vehicle and deployed in a chain in the direction of the shots being fired. Having gone literally a few dozen metres directly on the island, they were attacked by a large group of Chinese, who had risen from their ambush.

Bubenin's subordinates met the enemy, firing from a prone position. Having been repelled unexpectedly, the Chinese began to withdraw. When the last of them reached their positions, literally the entire ambush opened heavy fire against Bubenin's group. After some time, Chinese mortars struck here. The senior lieutenant was wounded and received a concussion, but he did not lose control of the battle – in fact, his subsequent actions were distinguished by surprise and valor.

Leaving in place several soldiers headed by Junior Sergeant Vasily Kanygin, Bubenin and four soldiers boarded the APC and moved around the island, making it to the rear of the Chinese ambush. Kanygin and his comrades rendered very timely assistance to Babansky's group. Vasily himself was a good sportsman-biathlon competitor, and an excellent shooter. Having taken up a comfortable position, Kanygin cold-bloodedly fired individual shots against the Chinese. At the same time, familiar with Kanygin's shooting talent, Private Nikolay Puzyrev collected ammunition from the dead and gave it to the junior sergeant.[13]

Private Petr Plekhanov was fighting to the left of Kanygin. Here is his account:

> At this time, men in white camouflage smocks (until this time we never had provocateurs in camouflage smocks) came toward us from behind breastworks and opened fire. We answered them with fire as well. I had 50 rounds, 25 of which I fired in long bursts, but then, having decided that I did not have enough rounds to last to the end of the battle, I began to fire single shots. An older, tall man commanded the provocateurs. He was dressed in a black fur coat. Upon the command of this man the provocateurs set off in a crowd in our direction, firing on the go from machine guns and carbines. However, when dead and wounded appeared among them, they gathered them up and withdrew behind the breastworks. Not even two minutes had passed before the provocateurs set off a second time. They made three attempts this way, but each time withdrew, collecting their wounded and dead.[14]

While Babansky's and Kanygin's groups were fighting, Bubenin circled the island and ended up in the rear of the Chinese ambush. The chief of the 1st border outpost himself stood at the heavy machine gun, and his subordinates opened the embrasures and fired from machine guns on both sides of the vehicle. The unexpected appearance of the Soviet APC and its fire caused definite confusion among the Chinese.

Thus, despite numerical superiority in personnel and firepower, the Chinese found themselves in an extremely unpleasant position: Babansky's and Kanygin's groups were firing on them from the island, and the manoeuvring APC was firing on them from the rear. However, Bubenin's vehicle also got hit: heavy fire from the Chinese riverbank and the island jammed the turret, the scope was broken, and the hydraulic system could not maintain the needed pressure in the punctured tires. The chief of the outpost himself received a new wound and concussion.

Veterans of the Damansky battles. Pavel Sikushenko (standing, first from the left), Vasily Kanygin (standing, second from the left) and Nikolay Puzyrev (standing, second from the right). (Military Museum of Hanoi, via Albert Grandolini)

Meanwhile, Bubenin was able to circle the island and take cover on the riverbank. At the very end of this raid the APC caught fire. The only one who was not wounded – APC driver-mechanic Arkady Shamov – pushed everyone out of the vehicle.

Bubenin telephoned Major Bazhenov, the duty officer of the border detachment, to report about the situation and request reinforcements. At this time, a GAZ-69 from the Kulebyakiny Hills Outpost had hurried to the place, carrying a group of soldiers headed by Sergeant Pavel Sikushenko. They brought a large quantity of ammunition, machine guns, and a grenade launcher. Inasmuch as Bubenin's APC had been taken out of action, the chief of the outpost had decided to use Strelnikov's APC, which was standing there.

Bubenin recalls:

> I called Private P. Kovalev, the driver of the 2nd outpost's APC.
> - Is the vehicle running?
> - Yes, sir.
> - Ammunition in place?
> - Yes.
> - Sikushenko, take around ten men, weapons, all the ammunition, and go in the APC. Leave 3-4 men to rig the machine gun belts. Sergeant Fadeyev is to stay here. Maintain communications and help the wounded. The rest – follow me![15]

The senior lieutenant and soldiers who had arrived took their places in the APC, after which they headed to the northern tip of Damansky. After this they moved along the front of the Chinese ambush, along the long, frozen bay.

The culmination of the fighting came at the moment when Bubenin succeeded in destroying the Chinese command post. That this had really happened became clear after the fighting, when a pile of broken field telephones, bloody bandages, etc. were found at the place of the ambush.

After the destruction of the command post, the Chinese began to leave their positions, carrying with them their dead and wounded. Obviously, several circumstances were telling here: the unforeseen and aggressive actions of the border guards, considerable losses among the Chinese, and loss of command and control.

The withdrawal of the Chinese was poorly organised and looked like a hasty retreat: mats, telephones, flasks, outer clothing, etc. had been thrown in the 'foxholes.' A large number of used individual medical kits were found there.

Having used up its ammunition, Bubenin's APC withdrew on the ice between the island and the Soviet riverbank. They stopped to take on board two wounded men – Nikolay Puzyrev and Anatoly Aniper. At that moment Chinese artillery hit the APC. Everyone inside was wounded.

Remarkably, although he had been wounded a third time, Bubenin and several soldiers once again set off for the island – this time on foot. He was taken from here to a hospital.

According to Chinese information, the battle ended at 11.50hrs. However, the surveillance log of the Soviet post on Mount Kafyla noted the time for the end of the battle differently: '12.50hrs. The Chinese began to withdraw in groups to the rear. They are dragging the wounded and dead off the island.' One more note follows a little later: '13.15hrs. The Chinese continue to move into the hills along the rear road.'

Close to 13.30hrs a helicopter landed not far from the island. On board was the Iman Border Detachment command, which before this had been located on manoeuvres 100 kilometres from where the events took place. A.D. Konstantinov recalls the following:

> In the morning we left for the manoeuvre area. The leadership – General Lieutenant Plotnikov, Deputy Commander of the Far Eastern Military District, and a group of generals and colonels – was at headquarters. We introduced ourselves and began to familiarise ourselves with the exercises. Demokrat Vladimirovich proposed that we wait for the tank regiment's counterattack and then go to Vvedenskoye.
>
> The tank regiment had somehow turned around badly, and Plotnikov commanded: "To the starting point!" This meant another couple of hours of waiting. Demokrat and I went to

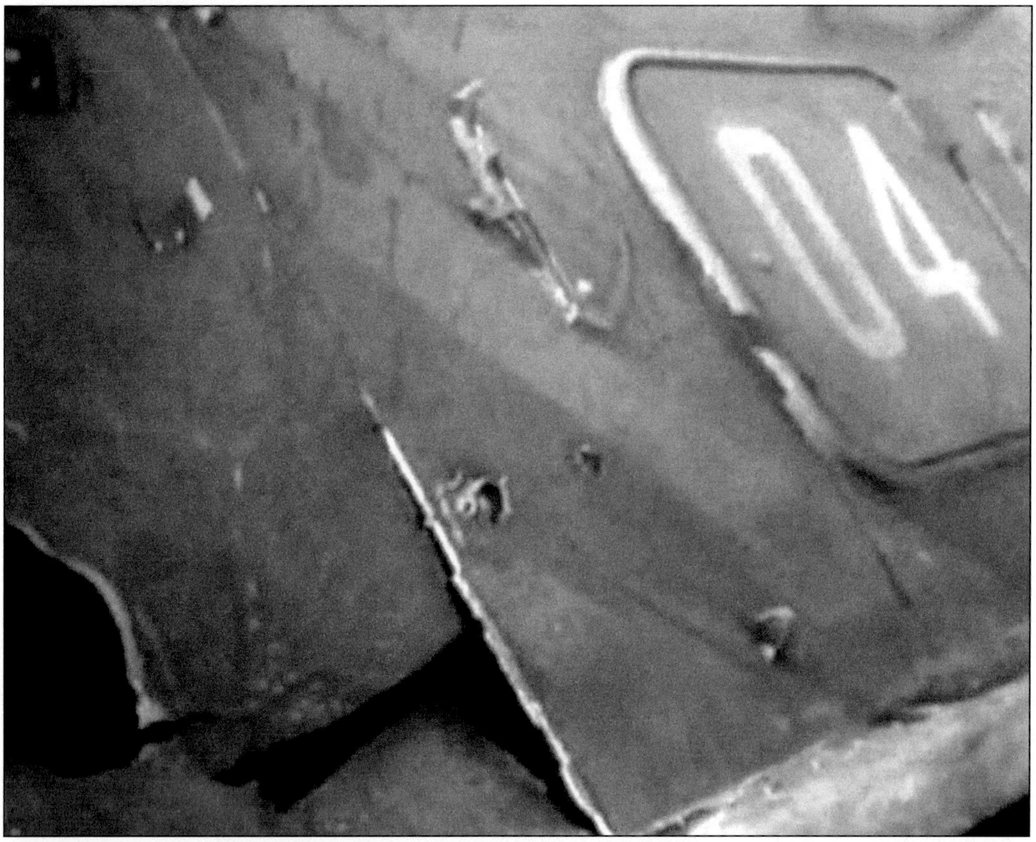

APC from the Nizhne-Mikhaylovka outpost, on which Bubenin attacked the Chinese ambush command post. (Military Museum of Hanoi, via Albert Grandolini)

V. Bubenin in the hospital. (from V.N. Volik)

taking my soldiers away from the exercises."[16]

Colonel D.V. Leonov, chief of the detachment, remained on the riverbank, while Lieutenant Colonel A.D. Konstantinov, chief of the political department, organised a search for the wounded and dead immediately on Damansky. A little later, reinforcements from neighbouring outposts – in particular, border guards from the Lastochka outpost, under the command of Senior Lieutenant V. Shorokhov – arrived at the scene of the events.

Local inhabitants – the brothers Genady and Dmitry Avdeyev and their namesake Anatoly – also took part in these events. They brought ammunition and machine guns on sleighs from the outpost and evacuated the wounded. Andrey Nikolayevich Tammes, an inhabitant of the village of Nizhne-Mikhaylovka, recalls the following:

> I was home on the day when the Chinese attacked Damansky. I was standing in the yard with a saw, when suddenly Mitka the beekeeper ran up to me and shouted: "Drop everything! War has begun!" I did drop everything. What's the sense of firewood when something like this is happening? I couldn't see from here what was there below, but my neighbours, the Avdeyevs, were bringing rounds to Damansky and saving the wounded from frostbite.[17]

the command post at the vehicle base, where Plotnikov and General Major Ishchenko, deputy chief of the military district's political directorate, were located. They offered us tea, and then the phone rang – their army communications. Plotnikov lifted the receiver: "So. Battle, yes?" He looked at Leonov: "Guard, it's for you." Leonov took the receiver, and his face immediately changed. He was speaking with the military district's duty officer in Khabarovsk, who had reported that fighting was underway at the Iman Border Detachment's 2nd outpost. There were dead and wounded. Demokrat reported to Plotnikov and Ishchenko: "I am

The wounded border guards were brought to the outpost, to the Lenin room, and military doctor Major V.I. Kvitko gave them first aid. Afterwards, a helicopter transported them to Filino, where a hospital was located.

Lidia Strelnikova also exhibited rare self-control that day. Having suddenly lost her husband, the young woman found the inner strength to make bandages and support the wounded border guards with kind words. And this even when she had two small children to take care of. She was subsequently awarded the Order of the Red Star.

As eyewitnesses attest, the dead border guards from Strelnikov's group were lying side-by-side – apparently, this is how death found them. There were no documents among the effects of the chief of the outpost (the Chinese had taken them), while Buinevich's documents were in place. The Chinese had removed the fur jackets and fur boots from Strelnikov and Buinevich.

The border guards who had taken part in the search broke up branches, lay the bodies down, and set off at attention to their riverbank. Yury Babansky, still heated from the battle, walked in front. The Chinese did not open fire, but only observed attentively the actions of the Soviet soldiers.

Nikolay Ivanovich Popov, a veteran of the fighting on Damansky Island, recalls the following:

> All the wounded were carried out to our spit of land, and then sent to the army hospital in Filino. The dead were then carried out and laid down in a row on this same spit. Finally, at around 17.00, they carried out Strelnikov's group, which had been lying in the channel after the shooting. At 23.00 GAZ-66s arrived; we lay the bodies of the dead in them and they set off for the outpost. We ourselves returned to the outpost after 01.00.[18]

Vladimir Prokhorovich Grechukhin, who in 1969 was a photo correspondent for the newspaper *Pogranichnik na Tikhom Okeane* [Border Guard on the Pacific Ocean], recalls the following:

> I found out about the battle on Damansky almost immediately, sometime around eleven in the morning. Three hours later I was already at the empty outpost. Of fifty border guards, eighteen remained alive. It was terrible to look at these living men. Next to them, in a hastily dug trench, lay the bodies of their friends, not yet even cold. Revenge blazed in the eyes of the living. However, from the district, or, more correctly, from Moscow, a strict order had arrived: do not get drawn into any provocation, do not engage in conflicts.[19]

Thus concluded the first battle on Damansky Island, on 2 March 1969. Fewer than two weeks remained before the dramatic denouement on 15 March.

4
THE FIRST AND THE LAST

The first victim of the 2 March 1969 battle was Chief of the Nizhne-Mikhaylovka Outpost Senior Lieutenant I.I. Strelnikov, or 'Black Ivan' as the Chinese called him. There are two opinions – one heroic and one prosaic – as to why he specifically earned this 'honour'. The first opinion is that this was because he acted decisively and uncompromisingly when driving out the Chinese from Soviet territory. The second opinion is that this was because in the winter he wore a black fur coat. However, even if the second variant was correct, in this case the word 'black' probably had a corresponding subtext from the first version.

Some Chinese sources also call Strelnikov 'the lame lieutenant'. Most likely there was a misunderstanding here, inasmuch as he was not lame. Possibly Strelnikov had been wounded in the leg during one of the clashes on the border, because of which he limped for a while, until he fully recovered.

Ivan Ivanovich Strelnikov was born on 9 May 1939 in the village of Bolshoi Khomutets, in the Dobrovsky District of the Ryazan *Oblast*. There were many children in the family: in addition to Ivan, the senior Strelnikovs brought up another nine children. In 1940 Strelnikov moved to a permanent residence in the village of Lyubchino, in the Okoneshnikovsky District of the Omsk *Oblast*. Here he finished fourth grade, and then went to the Okoneshnikovsky Middle School. Because he did not come from a rich family, after graduating eighth grade he had to earn money for his family instead of continuing with his education through the ninth and tenth years. He went to work at the 'Znamya Ilicha' collective farm, first as a record keeper and then as an assistant foreman.

In 1958 the time came for him to serve in the army, and he was drafted into the border guards. Strelnikov probably liked the service: he did not want to return to civilian life, and from that time his entire life was associated with the border.

Unfortunately, because he had not been able to continue his education through the 9th and 10th years, he was not eligible for advancement. However, he studied on his own, passed the 10th-year exams, and received his certification for this. After completing short-term officer courses in Moscow, he was conferred the rank of junior lieutenant and named chief of political affairs for the outpost.

As veterans who knew Strelnikov recall, he clearly felt a shortcoming in his general education, and, therefore, tried in every way possible to catch up to the more educated and cultured officers. He was an exceptionally strong-willed man, sometimes abrupt. At the same time, he distinguished himself by his honour and decency.

V. Bubenin describes his first meeting with Strelnikov as follows: 'Before me stood a rather young lieutenant, the same age as I, a little taller than I, lean, rangy, and fit. An open face with somewhat high cheekbones, his regular facial features expressed some kind of internal strength and confidence, and his large blue eyes were calm and kind.'[1]

Some publications express the opinion that Strelnikov's lack of the necessary education was one of the reasons for the unsuccessful beginning of the 2 March battle for the Soviet border guards. It is hard to agree with this point of view, inasmuch as in the conflict on Damansky Island the main thing was not education, but rather practical experience and good knowledge of the terrain. In the final analysis, the insignificant scale of the battle (in the geographic sense) required not strategists, but rather tacticians and men with practical experience. Ivan Strelnikov was just such a commander.

Strelnikov served as deputy for political affairs for a relatively short time; the next step in his officer career was as chief of the outpost. Apparently, the command valued the professional qualities of the young officer, who was best suited for work as a commander.

Strelnikov was married; with his wife, Lidia Fedorovna, he raised and educated his son Igor and his daughter Svetlana.

In one of the Pacific Ocean Border District's combat leaflets for 1969, the following was written about Strelnikov:

> For a long time the Chinese Maoists made provocative forays on the Soviet Damansky Island, which is located on the Ussuri River,

Junior Sergeant I. Strelnikov (right) with his friend. He was a model soldier, which is attested by the badges on his tunic (from left to right): 'Ready for Labour and the Defence of the USSR', the sportsman-athlete badge, 'Outstanding Border Guard', and Member of the Komsomol. (from V.N. Volik)

Strelnikov with his son Igor and daughter Svetlana. (from V.N. Volik)

On 2 March 1969, the Maoists committed a heinous crime. In the night, they made their way like thieves to Damansky Island, and, treacherously from an ambush, shot the brave communist, Senior Lieutenant Ivan Ivanovich Strelnikov, and his comrades-in-arms point-blank.

The Soviet border guards took revenge on the murderers. Only a few of the provocateurs remained alive.

By order of the Presidium of the Supreme Soviet of the USSR, Senior Lieutenant Ivan Ivanovich Strelnikov was posthumously conferred the title Hero of the Soviet Union for heroism and bravery.

on the border. They waved Mao quotation books, crudely cursed our border guards, and provoked them to retaliatory actions. However, the brave protectors of the Soviet state, under the command of the outpost chief, Senior Lieutenant Ivan Ivanovich Strelnikov, have demonstrated restraint and self-control. However raging the crowds of infuriated violators of the state border were, Ivan Ivanovich Strelnikov and his comrades-in-arms drove them out of our territory.

Before long the Chinese provocateurs began to appear on the island with poles, crowbars, and machine guns. Even in this situation Senior Lieutenant I.I. Strelnikov and his comrades-in-arms were victorious, without using weapons.

Ivan Strelnikov was the first border guard to be killed in the surprise attack by the Chinese on 2 March 1969. And Corporal Pavel Andreyevich Akulov was the last participant in the battle to perish, truly dying a martyr's death.

Late in the evening on 2 March, the procedure for identifying the dead took place at the Nizhne-Mikhaylovka outpost. The bodies of the border guards were carried to a large barn, and here the Soviet commanders, physicians, and photographers carried out their sombre work. Everything that had happened – faces covered in blood, the lack of daylight, etc. – had a most profound psychological effect on those present. That is why they even did not immediately discover the absence of Corporal Akulov. Under the circumstances that had developed, the disappearance of the border guard could mean only one thing – he had been taken prisoner.

Initially, Pavel Akulov had been drafted into the Soviet Army, where he was an SPG-9 grenade launcher gunner. Only after that was he transferred to the border guards. According to information from people who knew Pavel, he was a man of few words, even a bit reserved; that being said, however, he had the ability to interact with soldiers. It was this quality that was one of the main reasons Akulov was elected secretary of the Komsomol organisation at the Nizhne-Mikhaylovka outpost.

Gennady Mikhaylovich Zhestkov, who in 1969 was the Iman Border Detachment's assistant chief of the political department for Komsomol work, recalls a very noteworthy conversation with Akulov, which took place not long before the beginning of the events. In assessing the situation on the border, Akulov said that it might soon come to much blood. To the officer's question as to why he thought so, Akulov explained: 'Because the eyes of the Chinese look like they are drunk or stoned.'

On 2 March Akulov was in Rabovich's group. He was seriously wounded and, in fact, had been captured. Regarding why the Chinese had paid attention specifically to him, the border guards put forth two versions. The first version: when the alarm was sounded Akulov hurriedly put on a fur jacket with officer shoulder straps; therefore, the Chinese took him for an officer. It is possible that this happened, although it is not clear where a corporal could have taken an officer's fur jacket. Moreover, the Chinese had the opportunity of capturing one or two officers (I. Strelnikov and N. Buinevich) but did not do this. More likely, Akulov's outer clothing could have been newer, which attracted the attention of the Chinese. The second version: the Chinese mistook him for one of their own dead.

The fact is that on the battlefield the Soviet border guards discovered the body of a Chinese soldier. They brought him to the Soviet riverbank and buried him in the snow, placing a marker there. Thus, if the Chinese had kept strict records of their personnel, the second version could be considered completely plausible.

There is one more explanation, which can today be found in Chinese sources. It is said that the body of the dead soldier, whose name was Chen Jingli, was simply not noticed in the hurried Chinese withdrawal from Damansky Island. Cited as a contributing factor to what happened was the Chinese soldiers' use of camouflage capes, which made them difficult to see in the snow.

As for Akulov, practically nothing is known about his subsequent fate. In some articles it is written that the Chinese put the corporal in an iron cage and took him around the country, exhibiting him to the people as a 'Soviet revisionist'. Then, they say, the Maoists threw his disfigured body from a helicopter onto Soviet territory.

No one and nothing confirms the version with the cage, and as for the helicopter, that is pure fantasy. In fact, Akulov's body was returned to the Soviets in exchange for the remains of that very Chinese soldier who had been discovered on the island. The exchange took place at one of the outposts of the Kamen-Rybolovsky Border Detachment on 20 April 1969, that is, a month and a half after the battle. The choice of the place of exchange was probably determined by the fact that the border here was dry land.

An examination of the body showed that there were numerous wounds that had been received after the battle. An official medical report was prepared as a result of the discovery. One of the conclusions was that the corporal had been subjected to terrible torture (his sex organs had even been cut off) and died soon after he was captured.

Akulov's mother, Tatyana Illarionovna, who took part in the identification of the body, wrote the following in a letter to the border guards:

> I first walked up to his legs, and then to his head, and what did I see? His face was beaten severely, his body was very yellow, like akrikhin.[2] His nose, lips, and ears had been cut off. His nose had been plugged up, as if it weren't there. Netting had been placed in his mouth. There had been a severe blow to his head. An examination incision. And this was everything I could see. After I threw a sheet over him and I put a handkerchief into his hand, and I noticed a wart on his index finger, which convinced me that this was Pavel . . . His teeth had been pulled out. And they cut whatever could be cut out.[3]

Pavel Akulov was buried at the 2nd Border Outpost on 25 April 1969.

Chinese sources generally do not report anything about Akulov being a prisoner. Where was he? Why did they torture him? Who of the Chinese commanders or political figures decided his fate? In Beijing they know the answers to these and other questions. Probably those Chinese soldiers who by chance had contact with the prisoner – his guards, those who brought him his food, etc. – would have much to say. Only where are these witnesses to be found?

5
THE TWO SIDES' LOSSES: FACT AND FICTION

In the 2 March 1969 battle the Soviets lost 31 killed. It is this figure that was cited at the press conference held by the MFA of the USSR on 7 March 1969.

With the passage of time, some sources have begun to cite the figure of 32 killed. Obviously, this discrepancy is associated with Pavel Akulov, about whose fate nothing was known for some time. Documents confirm this assumption, inasmuch as on 27 March 1969 Colonel Mikhaylov, chief of the 4th staff department of the Red Banner Pacific Ocean Border District, signed a list of names of personnel combat losses in the battles of 2 March and 15 March. In the chart 'When and where Buried', there is a dash next to Akulov's name.

The following is an alphabetical list[1] of names of those who died on 2 March 1969:

- Corporal Pavel Andreyevich Akulov
- Senior Lieutenant Nikolay Mikhaylovich Buinevich
- Private Ivan Romanovich Vetrich*[2]
- Private Viktor Illarionovich Gavrilov*
- Corporal Gennady Mikhaylovich Davydenko
- Private Vladimir Nikolayevich Danilin
- Private Anatoly Grigoryevich Denisenko
- Sergeant Nikolay Timofeyevich Dergach
- Private Viktor Ivanovich Yegupov
- Sergeant Viktor Markiyanovich Yermalyuk*
- Private Aleksey Petrovich Zmeyev*
- Private Valentin Grigoryevich Zolotarev
- Private Vladimir Alekseyevich Izotov*
- Private Aleksandr Filimonovich Ionin*
- Private Vyacheslav Petrovich Isakov
- Private Grigory Aleksandrovich Kamenchuk
- Private Gavriil Georgiyevich Kiselev
- Junior Sergeant Nikolay Ivanovich Kolodkin
- Corporal Viktor Kharitonovich Korzhukov*

- Private Aleksey Nifantyevich Kuznetsov
- Junior Sergeant Mikhail Andreyevich Loboda
- Corporal Yevgeny Konstantinovich Mikhaylov
- Private Islamgali Sultangaleyevich Nasretdinov*
- Private Sergey Alekseyevich Nechay
- Private Gennady Sergeyevich Ovchinnikov
- Private Aleksandr Ivanovich Pasyuta
- Private Nikolay Nikolayevich Petrov
- Sergeant Vladimir Nikitovich Rabovich
- Senior Lieutenant Ivan Ivanovich Strelnikov
- Private Aleksey Nikolayevich Syrtsev*
- Private Aleksandr Fedorovich Shestakov
- Private Vladimir Mikhaylovich Shusharin.

Of the 32 men who died, 22 served at the Nizhne-Mikhaylovka Outpost, nine served at the Kulebyakiny Hills Outpost, and one (N. M. Buinevich) served in the border detachment.

Fifteen border guards were wounded in this battle. It is true that at first the number cited was 14; however, afterwards it was explained that Private Petr Velichko had hid his wound from the doctors and commanders so as not to abandon his comrades at such a crucial moment. Subsequently, it was clarified that he had been wounded by a mine fragment.

The authors of some articles about the Damansky events sometimes express their doubts that the above-mentioned list of dead border guards encompasses actual losses. They say that the true number of those who died was hidden from the Soviet people, and that, indeed, the number was much greater. It is hard to say what motivated the fans of such 'sensations' – a desire to show off their knowledge to others, or to once again disparage the Soviet past.

Therefore, it does not hurt to repeat once more: on 2 March 1969, 31 Soviet soldiers perished, and somewhat later POW Private Akulov died. This number is supported by specific names, ranks, posts, home addresses, etc. It is this information that must be demanded of those who proclaim other numbers: only then can any new information be examined seriously.

As for Chinese losses, the information regarding this is contradictory. It is bad enough that Chinese officials hide the true numbers, but some Russian authors also add to the confusion about this issue. Unfortunately, it is necessary to say that V.D. Bubenin cites the strangest figure in his memoirs. Describing the 2 March battle, the veteran writes: 'According to official information, we killed as many as 248 Chinese soldiers and officers on the island in a little more than two hours. It is not known how many we shot on the channel.'[3]

The number '248' that Bubenin suggests was widely disseminated in the pages of books, newspapers and journals, although it still would be clear, even to a layman, that, in principle, this could not be. The brevity of the battle, the unexpectedness of what happened for the Soviets, the limited amount of ammunition, the small number of border guards, and other such circumstances rule out inflicting such significant losses on the Chinese. It is possible that something would have been cleared up had Bubenin explained from which

Weapons and equipment of the Soviet border guards, captured by the Chinese on 2 March 1969. On the left can be seen I. Strelnikov's loudspeaker, the 'Kiev' motion picture camera that belonged to N. Petrov, and the 'Smena' and 'Zorky' cameras. (Chinese Internet)

Dead Chinese soldier who was found on the battlefield on 2 March 1969. Chinese sources say that his name was Chen Jingli. (photo from the archive of A.I. Glotov)

'official' sources he had obtained this information, but he is silent about precisely this.

By the way, analysing the results of the 2 March battle, the border detachment command estimated Chinese casualties to be around 100 men; this figure includes dead and wounded. If we take into account that, in normal battle, for each dead soldier there are several wounded, then one can say that the number of dead Chinese was in the range of 20–30 men. This estimated information corresponds with the number of graves on Memorial Square in the town of Baoqing, where the Chinese servicemen who died on Damansky Island are buried.

The following is a list of those Chinese who died in the 2 March battle (a total of 20 names):

- Yu Qingyang
- Chen Shaoguang
- Wang Qingrong
- Chen Mingduo
- Duo Jinrong
- Li Canrong
- Li Hongben
- Chen Lijian
- Xiang Wenbin
- Wen Dengjin
- Bai Zhicheng
- Chen Jingli
- Wang Shanyuan
- Lu Zhexiang
- Mei Yunxuan
- Zhou Guoshu
- Nong Yuping
- Li Zhongrong
- Guo Zhuni
- Xiang Shunguo.

In addition, in the cemetery there is the grave of serviceman Yao Junxiang, with the date of death given as 4 March 1969. Inasmuch as there were no clashes or exchanges of gunfire on 3 or 4 March, one can assume that Yao Junxiang died from wounds received in the 2 March battle.[4]

The number '248' that Bubenin introduced inspired several authors to irresponsibly say that it was on the island that Soviet border guards also found the bodies of dead Chinese. Moreover, some 'chronicles' go further, inventing completely fantastic numbers of Chinese losses. The following is a typical passage:

> The facts are that after the battle on the island was over, 248 bodies of PLA soldiers and officers were collected (and then sent to the Chinese). Generals Bubenin and Babansky are now more modest in their estimates of the dead Chinese. In a conversation with me three years ago, neither of them claimed a figure for Chinese losses that was greater than the officially recognised one, although it is understood that the Chinese managed to drag dozens of their dead to their own territory. In addition, the border guards successfully suppressed enemy fire positions that were detected on the Chinese bank of the Ussuri, so that losses for the attackers could easily have been 350–400 men.[5]

At this point, it is necessary to say the following: the authors had at their disposal a document that listed everything that was found at the location of the Chinese ambush after the 2 March battle. The entire text is provided here:

Chinese 'foxholes' on Damansky Island. Around 300 Chinese soldiers occupied positions here on the night of 2 March 1969. (Military Museum of Hanoi, via Albert Grandolini)

All this was found after the battle at the location of the Chinese ambush on Damansky: telephone, cable, bottles with vodka, and rusks. (Military Museum of Hanoi, via Albert Grandolini)

Used individual Chinese dressing packets found on Damansky after the battle on 2 March 1969. (Military Museum of Hanoi, via Albert Grandolini)

Inventory of the items, left by the Chinese servicemen on Damansky Island on 2 March 1969.

As a result of an examination of the terrain in the area of the armed provocation by the Chinese on 2 March 1969 by representatives of the Border Military Unit 2488 Lieutenant Colonel Aleksandr Dmitriyevich Konstantinov in the presence of Junior Lieutenant Nikolay Ivanovich Popov and Junior Lieutenant Mikhail Illarionovich Koleshnya, the following were discovered:

1) The corpse of a Chinese serviceman in warm field-type clothing, without a hat, with a laceration in the area of the back of the head on the right side. In the right pocket of the trousers there were two keys on a wire and crumbs of bread.
2) 7.62 mm SKS № Xa-9957-type carbine of Chinese manufacture with a bayonet – 1 item.
3) Small digging tools – 5 items.
4) Clips for carbines with cartridges – 3 items; without cartridges – as many as 20 pieces.
5) TAI-43 field telephones of Chinese manufacture – 3 items.
6) Black field cable of Chinese manufacture, up to 2,000 metres.
7) Spools for rolling cable, wooden – 5 items.
8) First aid kits of Chinese manufacture in factory packing and used during provocation – 50 items.
9) Army flasks: empty or full with alcohol – 10 items.
10) Bottles: empty, half-empty and full with alcohol, of Chinese manufacture.
11) Various mats (reed, wooden) – 25 items.
12) Various warm wear (hats, jackets, mittens) of Chinese manufacture.
13) Dry biscuits and other breads of Chinese manufacture.
14) A large number of Chinese grenade and mine fragments.
15) Cases for powder charges for firing from grenade launchers of Chinese manufacture.
16) Cartridge belt without cartridges for firing from a machine gun.
17) Straps of Chinese manufacture for carrying wounded servicemen – as many as 5 items.
18) Camouflage cloaks, white, of Chinese manufacture – 2 items.

There were no documents identifying the dead Chinese serviceman. All items of Chinese manufacture were packed and forwarded to military unit 2488.

Officer of Military Unit 2488
Lieutenant Colonel (Konstantinov)
In the presence of:
Junior Lieutenant (Popov)
Junior Lieutenant (Koleshnya)
17 March 1969

Thus, only one dead Chinese, not 248, was found on the battlefield. Nikolay Ivanovich Popov recalls the following:

> When making a sweep of the island on 2 March, from 14.00 to 18.00, I and a group of 19 men (I was the twentieth) moved from north to south, and at the end of a rampart (left, apparently, from the war) discovered the body of a Chinese, with the smell of alcohol coming out of his mouth and a laceration on the back of his head. A winter hat (treuh) was lying 50 centimetres from his head, and an XA-9957 carbine was lying 1 metre from his left leg. There were no rounds in the carbine; apparently they had all been fired. There were bread crumbs in his left pocket and two small keys (around 3 centimetres) on a yellow wire ring in his right pocket. He had nothing more with him. His uniform: a field-type jacket with pockets for magazines, and warm winter sneakers. His branch of service and specialty are unknown: he had no insignias.[6]

As was already mentioned, the body of the dead man was exchanged for Corporal Akulov's body.

The study of the cited document makes it possible to uncover a minor myth that was widely disseminated. The fact is that in their publications various authors show photographs of Chinese weapons allegedly found on the battlefield. In accordance with the inventory, the sole item of captured equipment was a carbine that was lying next to the dead Chinese soldier. As for the above-mentioned photographs, they show Chinese carbines and machine guns taken from the Chinese in the hand-to-hand fighting before 2 March. This is indicated by visibly damaged weapons – broken rifle stocks, bent barrels, etc.

Let us focus attention on the number of dressing packets. There was a total of 50 items, which means that the overall number of Chinese losses were, in fact, as many as 100 men killed and wounded (at present the Chinese say that they received 35 wounded men).

6
HORRIFIC

Some of the circumstances of the death of the Soviet border guards in the first battle on Damansky Island were announced by L.M. Zamyatin, head of the press department of the USSR MFA, at a press conference held at the MFA on 7 March 1969. It was then that for the first time words were said that aroused extreme indignation for Soviet citizens:

> During the provocation, the Chinese military committed incredibly brutal and cruel acts against the wounded Soviet border guards. Based on the on-site inspection and the conclusions of the medical commission, which examined the corpses of the dead Soviet border guards, it can be stated that the wounded were shot by the Chinese at close range [and/or] stabbed with bayonets. The faces of some of the dead border guards were distorted beyond recognition.[1]

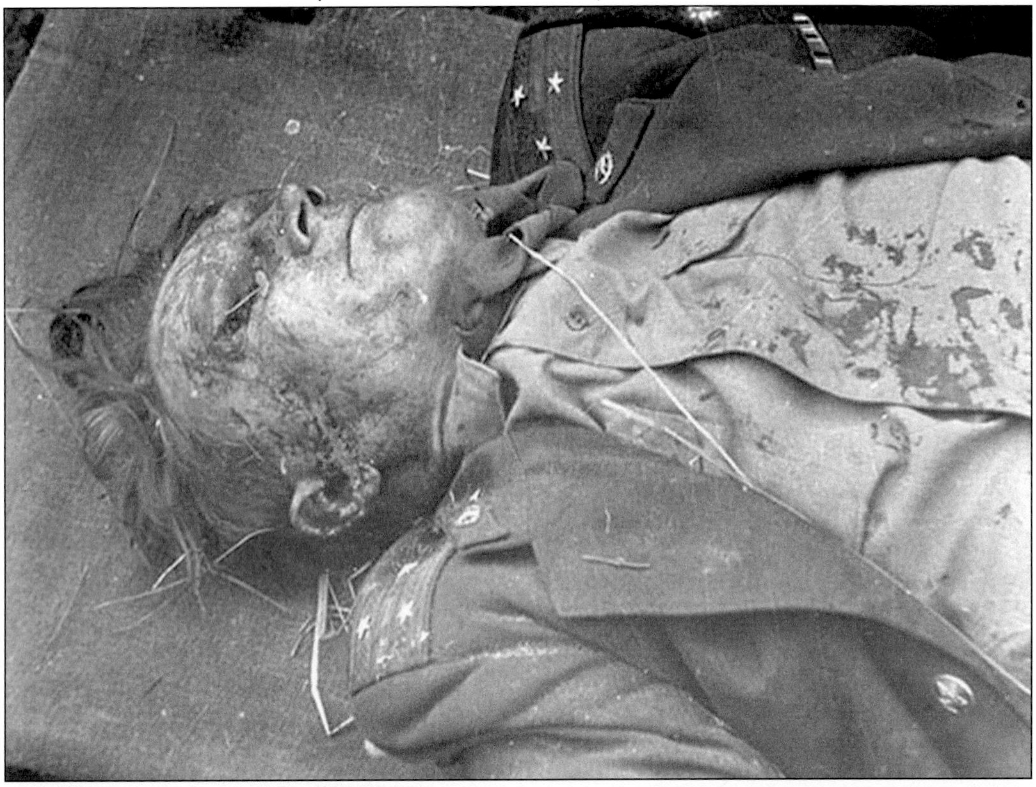

I. Strelnikov. (photo from archive of N.I. Popov)

N. Buinevich. (photo from archive of N.I. Popov)

On 8 March 1969 the leaders of the German Democratic Republic (GDR) received a note from their Moscow colleagues, which presented the course of events on Damansky Island.[2] The text of the note, for the most part, repeated Zamyatin's announcement. There were, however, some additions; for example, it said that clothing and shoes had been removed from some of the dead border guards.

As it happened, in their publications some irresponsible authors cited crazy 'details' of what had happened, as if competing as to whose description would be the most horrifying. Actually, the following is what really took place.

After the 2 March battle, all the dead border guards were moved to a large barn at the Nizhne-Mikhaylovka

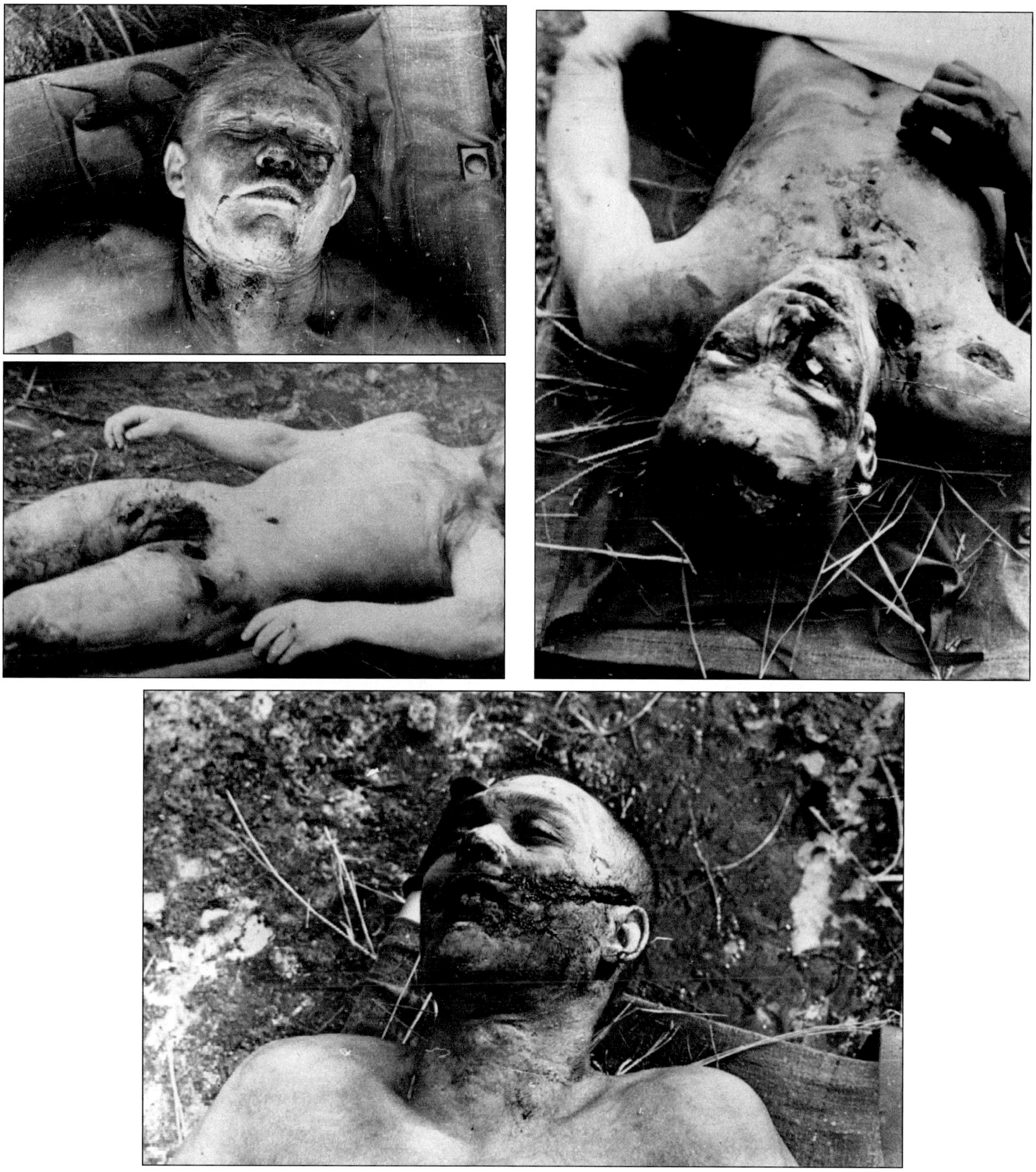

Soviet border guards who died on 2 March 1969. (photos from archive of N.I. Popov)

Outpost. Here a group of officers identified and drew up a medical examination certificate for the fallen warriors. Four men – Major of the Medical Service V.I. Kvitko, Lieutenant of the Medical Service B.Ya. Fotovenko, Lieutenant of the Medical Service N.I. Kostyuchenko, and Captain D.A. Petrov – signed the certificate. Below is the full text of the document:[3]

> Statement
> of the medical examination of the corpses of the servicemen of the military unit 2488, perished during repulsing of the armed intrusion of Chinese servicemen into the territory of the USSR 2 March 1969
>
> “ ” March 1969: Nizhne-Mikhaylovka
> The Commission of the Chief of the Military Medical Service, Major of Medical Service V.I. Kvitko, army doctors of the medical post Lieutenant of Medical Service V.Ya. Fotovenko, Lieutenant of Medical Service N.I. Kostyuchenko, and journalist D.A. Petrov examined 31 corpses of the servicemen of the military unit 2488; during the examination found the following:

1. Sergeant Yermalyuk Viktor Markiyanovich, Russian, born in 1948.

On the body there are multiple shrapnel wounds and traces of burns, and both lower extremities are amputated – probably, by shrapnel. Death came because of acute loss of blood.

2. Private Zmeyev Aleksey Petrovich, Russian, born in 1948.

On the body there are multiple shrapnel wounds, a shrapnel wound in the area of the left tibia. In the occipital area there is an entrance bullet hole from a point-blank shot. Death came because of brain damage.

3. Corporal Korzhukov Victor Kharitonovich, Russian, born in 1948.

There are bullet wounds in the chest area, lumbar area, and left shoulder. Death came because of chest injuries.

4. Private Izotov Vladimir Alekseyevich, Russian, born in 1949. Bullet wound in the chest area, signs of a blow with a blunt instrument to the anterior abdominal wall and the left hip (blow with a rifle butt). Death came because of damage to the abdominal organs.

5. Private Ionin Aleksandr Filimonovich, Russian, born in 1949.

Two gunshot wounds in chest area, crushing of the soft tissues and bones of the skull from a point-blank shot. Death came because of brain damage.

6. Private Nasretdinov Islamgali Sultangaleyevich, Tatar, born in 1949.

Bullet wound in the area of the right shoulder and the left half of the chest. Death came because of damage to the chest organs.

7. Private Vetrich Ivan Romanovich, Russian, born in 1949.

Shrapnel wound in the area of the left shoulder and multiple wounds with a cutting instrument (bayonet, knife) in the area of spine and neck. Death came because of acute loss of blood.

8. Private Gavrilov Viktor Illarionovich, Russian, born in 1950.

Bullet wound in the area of the left shoulder and chest. Death came because of damage to the chest organs.

9. Private Syrtsev Aleksey Nikolayevich, Russian, born in 1948. Bullet wounds in the area of the anterior abdominal wall and chest. Death came because of damage to the chest and abdominal organs.

10. Sergeant Rabovich Vladimir Nikitovich, Ukrainian, born in 1948.

Tangential wound to the left shoulder, penetrating chop wound in the area of forehead. Gunshot wound in the occipital region from a point-blank shot. Death came because of brain damage.

11. Private Nechay Sergey Alekseyevich, Russian, born in 1948.

Bullet wound in lumbar area, the chest area, and the right shoulder. Death came because of damage to the chest organs.

12. Private Pasyuta Aleksandr Ivanovich, Ukrainian, born in 1948.

Bullet wound to the left tibia. Lacerations (bayonet, knife) in chest area. Death came because of acute loss of blood.

13. Private Kamenchuk Grigory Aleksandrovich, Russian, born in 1949.

Multiple knife wounds in the chest area and anterior abdominal wall. Death came because of damage to the chest and abdominal organs.

14. Private Ovchinnikov Gennady Sergeyevich, Russian, born in 1948.

Multiple bullet wounds in the chest area, the right shoulder and the right hip. Death came because of damage to the chest organs.

15. Private Zolotarev Valentin Grigoryevich, Udmurt, born in 1949.

Bullet wounds in the area of the anterior abdominal wall. Lacerations of the neck (bayonet, knife), fracture of the skull bones with a blunt instrument (rifle butt). Death came because of brain damage.

16. Private Shusharin Vladimir Mikhaylovich, Russian, born in 1947.

Multiple bullet wounds in the chest area and the anterior abdominal wall. Death came because of damage to the chest and abdominal organs.

17. Junior Sergeant Loboda Mikhail Andreyevich, Russian, born in 1949.

Bullet wounds on the front surface of the neck, stab wounds and lacerations to the face and neck (bayonet, knife). Death came because of acute loss of blood.

18. Private Isakov Vyacheslav Petrovich, Russian, born in 1948.

Multiple shrapnel wounds in the upper extremities, bullet wound in the anterior abdominal wall, crush wound in occipital area. Death came because of brain damage.

19. Private Denisenko Anatoly Grigoryevich, Ukrainian, born in 1949.

Bullet wound in the chest. Gunshot wound to the face from a point-blank shot. Stab wounds and lacerations on the skull. Death came because of brain damage.

20. Private Shestakov Aleksandr Fedorovich, Russian, born in 1949.

Shrapnel wounds in the area of the knee, chest, and left shoulder. Chop wound in the area of the back of the head (pole, bayonet and knife). Death came because of brain damage.

21. Junior Sergeant Kolodkin Nikolay Ivanovich, Russian, born in 1948.

Bullet wounds in the area of the anterior abdominal wall and lower extremities. Fracture of the left shoulder, stab wound and lacerations (bayonet, knife) in the area of front surface of neck. Death came because of acute loss of blood.

22. Sergeant Dergach Nikolay Timofeyevich, Russian, born in 1948.

Bullet wound in the chest area; bullet wound to the back of the head from a point-blank shot. Death came because of brain damage.

Designed immediately after the Korean War, the Mil Mi-4 was a relatively large helicopter patterned along the layout of the Sikorsky H-19 Chickasaw (including the engine position in front of the cockpit), in comparison to which it proved capable of lifting more weight. The first examples entered operational service in 1953; manufactured in large numbers, they became the backbone of the Soviet Army Aviation. The example shown here was a Mi-4A, primarily used as an assault helicopter and armed with a machine gun installed in an under-fuselage turret. It was painted in dark olive green on upper surfaces and sides and light admiralty grey on undersurfaces, as usual, but had its bort applied in yellow, instead of the more common red. (Artwork by Peter Penev)

The GAZ-69 was a basic light off-road, four-wheel-drive vehicle of the Soviet Army. Developed since 1947 to replace older GAZ-67s and Willys Jeeps, it was in production from 1953 until 1972. Shown is the basic variant which had only a pair of doors and a canvas top and upper sides as standard: the subsequent GAZ-69A had four doors, folding canvas top and two rows of seats. As usual for all Soviet military vehicles it was painted in dark olive green and wore only a bare minimum of insignia (mostly reduced to its licence plate). (Artwork by David Bocquelet)

The BTR-60 was the first in an entire series of eight-wheeled armoured personnel carriers designed for the Soviet Army. Initially meant to replace the BTR-152, it entered service in the form of an open-topped variant: however, in 1956-57 the GenStab made the decision to convert all rifle- and mechanised divisions into motorised rifle divisions and thus a new variant came into being with a roofed-in combat compartment, designated BTR-60PA. When a turret armed with the KPVT 14.5mm heavy machine gun and a PKT 7.62mm machine gun was added on the top, in 1966, the definitive version came into being as the BTR-60PB. Several vehicles of the border troops became involved in the clashes for Damansky Island, including the example illustrated here. All were painted in dark olive green overall, and only wore their 'bort' numbers in white. (Artwork by David Bocquelet)

This soldier of the Soviet Border Guard is shown wearing the traditional synthetic *Ushanka* hat, *Valenki* boots, and the thick Sz52 coat, made of sheepskin. Usually issued only to officers deployed on other parts of the Soviet border, this outfit was issued to the Border Guard troops along much of the border with China, protecting them well against the extreme cold of the local area. His gear consists of a leather belt with the Red Star on the buckle, an old-model magazine-pouch, and a 6x3 Type 1 bayonet (with its characteristic wire-cutter sheath). His firearm is a Kalashnikov AKM assault rifle. (Artwork by Anderson Subtil)

This sergeant of the Soviet Border Guard is shown as on a patrol during the conflict on Damansky Island, equipped with the *Telogreika* padded uniform from the period of the Second World War, but still in widespread use during the 1960s. His rank is shown on shoulder straps, while the service branch is indicted by collar patches, both of which were in green, the colour used by the Soviet Border Guards. He wears a *Ushanka* cap with the Red Star on the front flap. His uniform is completed by the classic Soviet *Kirza* boots, and a pouch for magazines for his AKM assault rifle. (Artwork by Anderson Subtil)

General Major V. K. Nesov, commander of the 135th Motorised Rifle Division, shown wearing the M-1954 winter overcoat for generals and marshals of the Soviet armed forces, which was intended for use at parades and on daily duty alike. The overcoat featured red piping along the collar and the sleeves, showing his general rank. His shoulder boards were grey with one gold bullion star for his rank. His *Papakha* hat, made of lambskin, had a red top, and was reserved for senior officers of the Soviet Army. The brown belt with crossed strap had a large golden buckle (also reserved for generals), while his boots were made of high-quality leather, and had a white leather lining. (Artwork by Anderson Subtil)

All the personnel of the People's Liberation Army involved in clashes on Damansky Island wore the Type-65 winter suit, and caps with brown fur flaps, closely resembling the Soviet-made *Ushanka*. This illustration shows an official, probably a political commissar (Zhengwei), recognisable as being armed only with a Type-54 'Black Star' pistol, a Chinese copy of the Soviet Tokarev TT-30. Notably, he holds a copy of the "Little Red Book" in his hand, and has a pin-badge showing Mao Zedong on his left breast pocket. (Artwork by Anderson Subtil)

Probably a soldier of the PLA Border Guards, this infantryman is shown wearing the Type-65 winter suit with a simpler and lighter hat with ear-flaps, the so-called 'ChiCom' chest pouch rig for magazines, and his Type-56 rifle – the Chinese variant of the Soviet SKS. (Artwork by Anderson Subtil)

A typical PLA infantryman of 1969, wearing a *Ushanka* made of synthetic fleece (here shown with ear-flaps down) and including a snow-white camouflage cape atop of his Type-65 winter suit. During the times of the Cultural Revolution, it was a popular practice for the PLA troops to wear the Mao pin-badge (shown inset), which included the slogan 'Service to the People' at its base. His weapon is the Chinese-made 7.62x39mm Type-56 assault rifle (probably the initial version, still without attachments for a bayonet, which is characteristic for this Chinese copy of the AK-47), and his webbing with four magazine pouches. (Artwork by Anderson Subtil)

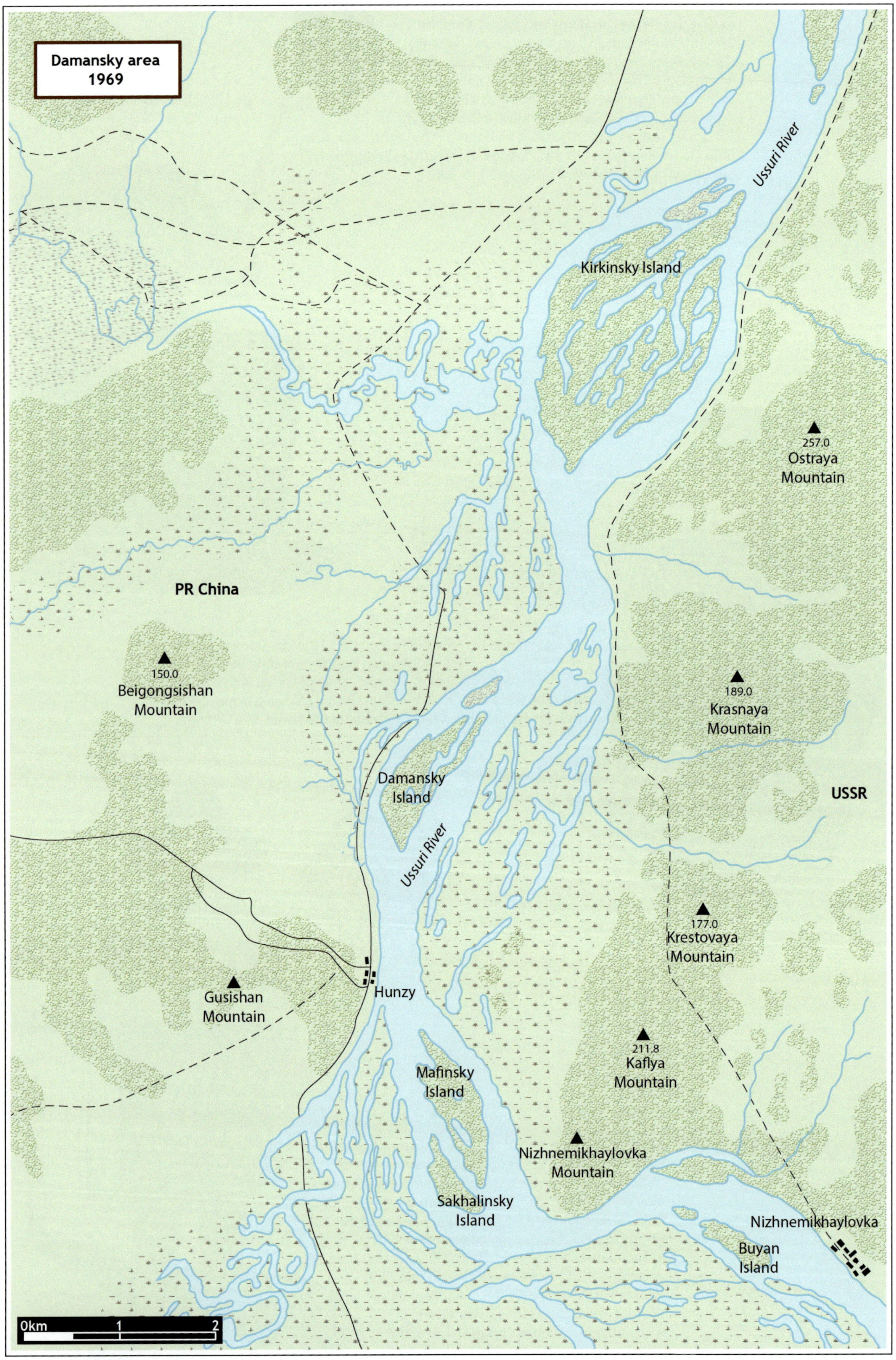

(Map by George Anderson)

23. Corporal Mikhaylov Yevgeny Konstantinovich, Russian, born in 1948.

Bullet wounds in the chest area and anterior abdominal wall. Shrapnel wounds in the pelvic area. Death came because of damage to the chest and abdominal organs.

24. Corporal Yegupov Viktor Ivanovich, Russian, born in 1947.

Bullet wound to the left shoulder and left hip. Stab wound and lacerations (bayonet, knife) in the temporal area. Death came because of brain damage.

25. Private Kiselev Gavriil Georgiyevich, Russian, born in 1950.

Bullet wound in the chest area and right upper extremity. Stab wound and lacerations in the skull area. Death came because of brain damage.

26. Corporal Davydenko Gennady Mikhaylovich, Russian, born in 1947.

Gunshot fracture of the right shoulder, lacerations (bayonet, knife) in the area of front surface of neck. Bullet wound in the occipital area. Death came because of brain damage.

27. Private Kuznetsov Aleksey Nifantyevich, Russian, born in 1948.

Perforating bullet wounds to chest and pelvis. Death came because of damage to chest organs.

28. Private Petrov Nikolay Nikolayevich, Russian, born in 1947.

Shrapnel wounds to the right tibia and in the left groin area, bullet wounds to the right shoulder and hip, stab wounds and lacerations in the skull area. Death came because of brain damage.

29. Private Danilin Vladimir Nikolayevich, Russian, born in 1950.

Bullet wounds to the upper extremities and head. Death came because of brain damage.

30. Senior Lieutenant Strelnikov Ivan Ivanovich, Russian, born in 1939.

Bullet wounds to lower extremities, bullet wound in facial area. Death came because of brain damage.

31. Senior Lieutenant Buinevich Nikolay Mikhaylovich, Russian, born in 1944.

Gunshot wounds to lower extremities, and chest and skull. Death came because of damage to chest organs and brain damage.

On almost all the corpses there are traces of injuries and mutilations, inflicted with cutting and heavy blunt instruments while they were still alive. Nineteen men perished because of injuries inflicted by bayonet (knife), rifle butt, and/or point-blank shots fired after the injured were already in a helpless state, after having received a bullet or shrapnel wound:

1. Private Zmeyev Aleksey Petrovich, after being wounded by shrapnel, was killed by a point-blank shot.

2. Private Izotov Vladimir Alekseyevich, after being wounded, was killed by a blow from a rifle butt.

3. Private Ionin Aleksandr Filimonovich, after being wounded by a bullet, was killed by a point-blank shot to the head.

4. Private Vetrich Ivan Romanovich, after being wounded in the left shoulder, was killed by bayonet (knife) blows in the area of the spine and neck.

5. Sergeant Rabovich Vladimir Nikitovich, after being wounded, was killed by a bayonet (knife) blow in the area of forehead and a shot to the back of the head.

6. Private Pasyuta Aleksandr Ivanovich, after being wounded in the leg, died from several bayonet (knife) blows in the chest area.

7. Private Zolotarev Valentin Grigoryevich, after being wounded in the stomach, was killed by bayonet (knife) blows and by a rifle butt to the head.

8. Junior Sergeant Loboda Mikhail Andreyevich, after being wounded, was killed by bayonet (knife) blows in the face and neck area.

9. Private Isakov Vyacheslav Petrovich, after being wounded, was killed by blow from a rifle butt to the head.

10. Private Denisenko Anatoly Grigoryevich, after being wounded, was killed by bayonet (knife) blows and a shot to the head.

11. Private Shestakov Aleksandr Fedorovich, after being wounded in the leg, was brutally killed by a bayonet (knife) blow to the back of the head.

12. Junior Sergeant Kolodkin Nikolay Ivanovich, after being wounded, received a broken arm and was killed by a bayonet (knife) blow to the neck.

13. Sergeant Dergach Nikolay Timofeyevich, after being wounded, was killed by a shot to the back of the head.

14. Private Yegupov Viktor Ivanovich, after being wounded, was killed by a bayonet (knife) blow to the temporal area.

15. Private Kiselev Gavriil Georgiyevich, after being wounded, was killed by a bayonet (knife) blow to the head.

16. Corporal Davydenko Gennady Mikhaylovich, after being wounded, was killed by a point-blank shot to the head.

17. Private Petrov Nikolay Nikolayevich, after being wounded, was brutally killed by a blow from a rifle butt to the head.

18. Senior Lieutenant Strelnikov Ivan Ivanovich, after having received several bullet wounds, was killed by a shot to the face.

19. Senior Lieutenant Buinevich Nikolay Mikhaylovich, after being wounded, was killed by a shot to the chest.

Mayor of Medical Service, (Kvitko)
Lieutenant of Medical Service, (Fotovenko)
Lieutenant of Medical Service, (Kostyuchenko)
Captain, (Petrov)

The original Chinese caption reads 'Soldiers of the Soviet revisionist clique throw themselves on the Chinese fishermen and beat them up'. (Chinese Internet)'

The original Chinese caption reads 'The new tsars of the Kremlin are a horde of out-and-out social-fascists. This Chinese fisherman has been injured by the beating he received from the Soviet hoodlums'. (Chinese Internet)

The original Chinese caption reads 'This Soviet revisionist hoodlum is beating up a Chinese teenage lad'. (Chinese Internet)

The original Chinese caption reads 'Cruel and barbarous, they turn a military dog on Chinese fishermen'. (Chinese Internet)

The actions of the Chinese regarding the wounded Soviet border guards are one of the most heinous war crimes, which is subject to severe condemnation and punishment. This fact will always remain an indelible blight in the history of the PLA, especially because in 1956 the PRC ratified the Geneva Conventions for the protection of victims of war (including those wounded on the battlefield). Having violated these agreements, the Chinese servicemen and their leaders became war criminals, to whose acts the statute of limitations does not apply.

The text of the medical commission's certificate reflects some details of the 2 March battle that were previously unknown. For example, from the certificate it follows that the Chinese finished off some of the wounded border guards not only in Strelnikov's and Rabovich's groups, but also in Bubenin's group. According to the certificate, this was specifically how I. Vetrich, A. Zmeyev, V. Izotov, and A. Ionin died. This likely means that, having fought against the Chinese, Bubenin's soldiers began at some time to crawl back to the eastern bank of the island, and the wounded that were left behind in the confusion were discovered by the attacking Chinese and killed off.

Another fact: there were only knife wounds on the body of G. Kamenchuk, with no traces of his having been killed off. This possibly indicates that he was in Strelnikov's group, which had come close to the Chinese. In any case, it is difficult to imagine a situation in which such wounds could have been inflicted, had Kamenchuk been in Babansky's or Rabovich's groups.

The question of how to explain the barbaric actions of the Chinese regarding the wounded Soviet soldiers lies, perhaps, in the field of psychology. However, there is one explanation that is obvious even for laymen: the issue lies in the misleading propaganda to which the entire Chinese population was subjected. There is much evidence of this: one such piece is the pamphlet, 'Down with the New Tsars!' published in China in 1969.[4] For example, the pamphlet cites a photo that depicts a Chinese boy attempting to match strength with a Soviet border guard. The impression is that the boy is trying to budge an adult from his place, but the pamphlet puts it differently: 'This Soviet revisionist hoodlum is beating up a Chinese teenage lad' (by the way, it would be interesting to know who brought a child to the border and why). Another photograph is captioned: 'Chinese fishermen killed by the Soviet revisionist renegade clique's armoured cars'; here is a close-up of the faces of the dead. Or there is another photo – a crowd on the ice of the border river, common for that time, but the Chinese propagandists see much more: 'Soldiers of the Soviet revisionist clique throw themselves on the Chinese fishermen and beat them up.' And here is a photograph in which two border guards are taking away a Chinese citizen who came onto Soviet territory. The commentary: 'The new tsars of the Kremlin are a horde of out-and-out social-fascists. This Chinese fisherman has been injured by the beating he has received from the Soviet hoodlums.' And so on, and so forth. The two photographs at the top of the next page are from the above-mentioned pamphlet.

It is obvious that, as a result of such daily 'ideological work' even the calmest and kindest people quickly turned into fierce

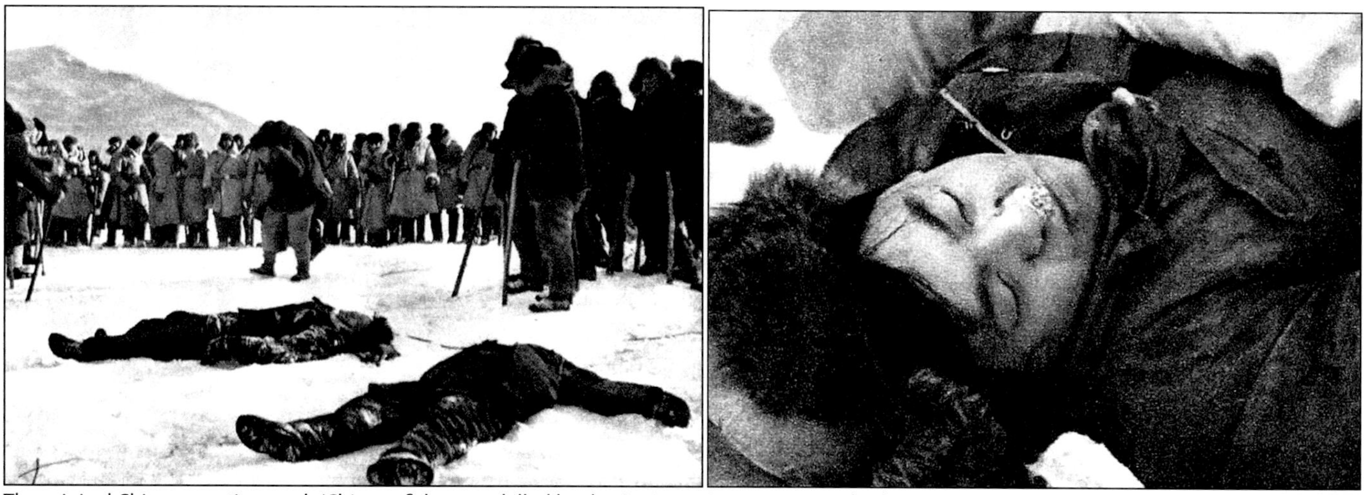

The original Chinese caption reads 'Chinese fishermen killed by the Soviet revisionist renegade clique's armoured cars'. (Chinese Internet)

enemies of the Soviet Union, burning with one desire – revenge. Therefore, the lion's share of the guilt for what happened is borne by the political organs of the Chinese Army, who mindlessly carried out the instructions of their leadership to foment hatred toward the Soviet people.

7
WHO SHOT FIRST?

The Chinese point of view regarding the events of 2 March 1969 is based on the conviction that the Soviets fired first. The phrase 'The Soviets were the first to open fire' has been repeated many times in many Chinese articles, books, memoirs and films about the war on Damansky Island. Then they say that the PLA soldiers were forced to launch 'a counterattack in self-defence' – this wording also drifts from one Chinese publication to another.

On 2 March the Soviet ambassador in China was called to the PRC's MFA, where he was handed a note of protest with the following content:

> Note of the Ministry of Foreign Affairs
> Of the People's Republic of China
> To the Soviet Embassy in China
> March 2, 1969
>
> On the morning of 2 March 1969, Soviet frontier guards intruded into the area of Chenpao Island, Heilungkiang Province, China, and killed and wounded many Chinese frontier guards by opening fire on them, thus creating an extremely grave border armed conflict. Against this, the Ministry of Foreign Affairs of the People's Republic of China is instructed to lodge the strongest protest with the Soviet Government.
>
> At 09.17 hours on 2 March, large numbers of fully armed soldiers, together with four armoured vehicles and cars, sent out by the Soviet frontier authorities, flagrantly intruded into the area of Chenpao Island which is indisputable Chinese territory, carried out blatant provocations against the Chinese frontier guards on normal patrol duty and were the first to open cannon and gun fire, killing and wounding many Chinese frontier guards. The Chinese frontier guards were compelled to fight back in self-defence when they reached the end of their forbearance after their repeated warnings to the Soviet frontier guards had produced no effect. This grave incident of bloodshed was entirely and solely created by the Soviet authorities. It is another grave new crime perpetrated by the Soviet authorities which have long been deliberately encroaching upon China's territory, carrying out armed provocations and creating ceaseless incidents of bloodshed.
>
> The Chinese Government firmly demands that the Soviet Government punish the culprits of this incident and immediately stop its encroachment upon China's territory and its armed provocations, and reserves the right to demand compensation from the Soviet side for all the losses suffered by the Chinese side. The Chinese Government once again sternly warns the Soviet Government: China's sacred territory brooks no violation; if you should wilfully cling to your reckless course and continue to provoke armed conflicts along the Sino-Soviet border, you will certainly receive resolute counter-blows from the Chinese people; and it is the Soviet Government that must bear full responsibility for all the grave consequences arising therefrom.[1]

When reading this document two circumstances are immediately apparent. Firstly, the Chinese note is literally shocking in the cynicism with which the organisers and masterminds of the bloodshed attempt to act as the accusers. After all, this document was probably examined and corrected by the higher leadership of the PRC, who were aware of absolutely all the details of what had taken place. Therefore, it is completely fitting to speak not only about the obvious costs of Chinese politics in the time of the 'cultural revolution' but also about the extremely low ethical qualities of China's leadership at that time.

Secondly, the fact that many phrases in this note, as well as those that followed, are reminiscent of a similar Soviet document draws attention to itself. It seems as if Chinese diplomats used a note from the Soviet government as a template for framing their answer. Probably they were in a big hurry.

Picture from a Chinese comic book. The 'Exploit of Zhou Dengguo'. (Chinese Internet)

In the foreground, 'hero' Zhou Dengguo, who killed I. Strelnikov with the machine gun he is holding. It is quite probable that it was he who fired the first shot on 2 March 1969. (Chinese Internet)

The next day the newspaper *Renmin Ribao* (*The People's Daily*) reported about the events on the border, repeating the text of the note.[2]

The PLA general staff prepared a brief information report about the events on Damansky for high-level party leaders. The following shows how the events looked through the eyes of Chinese generals:

> At 8.40hrs on 2 March, our border patrol of 30 soldiers went to Zhenbao Island in two groups to carry out their duties. The moment they set off, the Soviet revisionists discovered them. They dispatched one truck, two armoured vehicles, one command car, and about 70 soldiers from two different directions to encircle our soldiers. At 9.17hrs, ignoring our warnings, the enemy opened fire on our soldiers. Our soldiers were forced to begin a counterattack in self-defence. The enemy suffered heavy casualties. Our troops in the second tier fired as soon as they heard the gunshots, eliminating seven enemy soldiers immediately. At 9.50hrs, the battle ended successfully. The enemy's casualties totalled [*sic*] over 60, including more than 50 deaths. One armoured vehicle, one command car, and one truck on the enemy side were destroyed; another armoured vehicle was damaged.[3]

In reading this text, a fantastic interweaving of truth and fiction can be found. For example, the number of pieces of Soviet equipment and their types are truthfully indicated, and the overall numbers of border guards taking part in the battle are specified almost correctly. One can also probably trust the chronological information (of course, with a correction to Peking time). The main thing, however, for the sake of which this note was written, was 'ignoring our warnings, the enemy opened fire against our soldiers'.

The authors communicated with the young generation of Chinese and discussed this theme with them. As a rule, young people either generally know nothing about these events or know the minimum – just that 'the Soviets were the first to open fire' and then 'a counterattack in self-defence' followed. When you begin to tell them about the actual course of events, this causes genuine amazement – so strongly have the above-mentioned 'postulates' been embedded in their heads.

Of course, one can argue until one is blue in the face about who shot first. However, as of yet no one has presented documented evidence, and the testimony of eyewitnesses is always doubtful. Strictly speaking, on the Soviet side there is only one such eyewitness – Gennady Serebrov; as for Chinese witnesses, they are like ghosts: their memoirs sometimes appear for public review, but there is no way to see them in person (or in a photograph). This probably means that the Chinese authorities fear that their veterans might be drawn into an open discussion of the question, since they rightly assume that they might say something that does not conform to the established viewpoint.

Thus, the situation with witnesses is difficult. Nevertheless, the authors have the audacity to state that irrefutable evidence exists about who shot first.

To begin, let us ask some rhetorical questions for those who still assume that 'the Soviets were the first to open fire'.

As is known, run-ins between Chinese and Soviet servicemen occurred regularly on Damansky Island; however, the matter never went as far as shooting. Here, however, when the Chinese had carefully prepared the ambush on the island, outfitted positions on their riverbank, brought up artillery and mortars, and then sent a group of men to lure the Soviet border guards into the trap, the Soviet soldiers suddenly 'fired first'? This, despite the fact that for each Soviet soldier there was a minimum of 10 Chinese?

Today, no researcher (including the Chinese) disputes the fact that on the night of 2 March 1969 a special detachment of the PLA covertly came to Damansky to organise an ambush. The act performed by the Chinese unambiguously defines the very word 'ambush'. For example, here is how the *Soviet Military Encyclopaedia* defines the term: 'a method of troop action in which troops, deploying covertly, await an enemy and then **suddenly** [emphasis is the authors'] attack him for the purpose of killing and capturing prisoners, documents and models of weapons and military equipment.'[4] Thus, admitting the organisation of an ambush, it follows that a surprise attack is admitted as well. No ambush awaits the first shot from the enemy; the point of an ambush is precisely to catch the enemy by surprise. From this point of view, the actions of the Chinese seem completely logical: having allowed the Soviet border guards to approach at a minimum distance, the Chinese, in fact, shot Strelnikov's and Rabovich's group at close range with concentrated fire. So how in this case could the Soviet soldiers have shot first?

On 2 March the Soviet border guards moved in the direction of the Chinese in two groups. No one from Rabovich's group could have shot first, inasmuch as the PLA soldiers were lying behind a rampart, and up to the final moment it was physically impossible for the border guards to detect the Chinese ambush. Strelnikov's group also could not have fired: Nikolay Petrov's photography is evidence of this. Indeed, Petrov calmly recorded what was happening, using a motion picture camera and camera for taking still photos, inasmuch as he did not suspect what would happen in the next instant.

The circumstances of the beginning of the battle demonstrate the clear intentions of the Chinese to kill as many Soviet soldiers as possible. Not firing on them, not taking prisoners, but specifically killing them. Why? The answer is obvious: so that no witnesses to the crime would remain. After all, in that case the Peking propagandists could invent practically any scenario about what had happened. It is true that the Chinese made an unforgiveable 'blunder' here: Private Gennady Serebrov was alive, and he related what had actually happened.

And how does one explain the strange correlation of casualties on the Soviet side – 31 border guards killed on the battlefield and 15 wounded? After all, the experience of all armed conflicts and wars shows that the number of wounded in a typical battle substantially exceeds the number of dead. For example, in the subsequent new clash on 15 March, there were several wounded Soviet soldiers for each one who died. What is going on here? What is going on is the fact is that on 15 March the Soviets expected the Chinese attack, as opposed to the surprise attack by the Chinese on 2 March.

Here is one more detail: the precise chronology of the battle cited by an unknown Chinese person. This means that he knew about the operation that was being prepared and, moreover, he was ordered to deal with specifically this matter. As for the Soviet veterans, not one of them could cite the exact time for any particular moment of the battle.

The question of who began the shooting on Damansky Island, in the opinion of Chinese researchers, is a curious one. It should be mentioned that the political realities of the PRC do not always allow them to express themselves completely openly, inasmuch as undue openness may be punished. For this reason Chinese historians at home prefer only to cite various official announcements and assessments without casting doubt on their veracity, even when there are apparent inconsistencies and obvious questions arise.

The style of the narrative changes noticeably, however, if the Chinese experts are taking part in joint work with Western scholars or are publishing in foreign sources. In this case they demonstrate much greater objectivity in their discussions, although they do not forget what reaction the PRC authorities may have regarding their conclusions. Consequently, Chinese researchers try to avoid getting deeply involved in the military aspect of the matter and do not pose – at least in discussions – questions that may be critical of the official interpretation of the events that occurred. Instead, they prefer discussions on general political themes, the conduct of which are never-ending and without any risk of their being accused of a lack of patriotism. A typical example of this approach is the often-cited article by Yang Kuisong, which acknowledges that 'it was the Chinese who initiated the March 1969 border conflict with the Soviets... it seems likely that the Zhenbao Island Incident was indeed initiated by the Chinese side.'[5] Judging by everything, Yang Kuisong understood that the events of 2 March 1969 began with the surprise firing on Soviet border guards, but he lacks the courage to say that this was a surprise ambush of the Soviet border guards. In addition, several times he uses the rather vague word 'initiated' which anyone can interpret as he wishes.

Professor Li Danhui, another Chinese author, goes even further. This is how she proposes to treat the question of the first shot on Damansky: 'The principal issue associated with the armed conflict consists not of who was the first to begin preparing for the strike and not from whose side the first shot resounded... From the viewpoint of history, the key question is the time selected for delivering the strike.'[6]

It is apparent that the professor also understands who the first was to pull the trigger, but she cannot bring herself to tell the truth. Therefore, she proposes that this fact that is unpleasant for the Chinese be simply forgotten, and that instead of a detailed study of what occurred, we occupy ourselves with discussions of the historical scale, so loved by university professors. That being said, in her article Li Danhui inexplicably combines the responsibility of the Chinese authorities for the bloodshed on the border with denunciations of the Soviets for some kind of 'provocations'.

A completely different approach can be observed with American researchers – practical people who prefer clearly posed questions and clear answers. For example, Lyle Goldstein in one of his works rejects any downplaying of the importance of the question about the first shot, and unconditionally blames the Chinese military for what happened.[7]

Another couple of facts merit attention, the confirmation of which can be found on the Chinese internet by anyone who wants to.

In the museum the Chinese built on the former Damansky Island there is a display with photographs of the 'heroes' and a description of their 'exploits'. To illustrate, pictures are presented that artistically demonstrate the 'exploit' itself. The previously-mentioned Zhou Dengguo is depicted shooting Soviet border guards with a machine gun, among whom it is easy to recognise I. Strelnikov. In a Chinese comic book published in 1969 there is one more picture, boasting of the act performed by Zhou Dengguo. As they say, 'a picture is worth a thousand words'.

But now the main thing. The Chinese had prepared very well for battle. They had forgotten nothing, including several film makers, who continuously shot on camera what was happening, 'for history' so to speak. There exists no small quantity of unique film taken by the Chinese and completely accessible to anyone. For example, in Chinatowns in the US and Canada you will be kindly offered sets of discs with documentary films about every possible armed conflict in which the PLA participated – from the Korean War to clashes with Vietnam in 1984. There is even a two-hour film about Damansky. It is not difficult to find this film on the internet.

Some time ago two curious Chinese photographs were found on the internet. The first one depicted the arrival of Babansky's group. It is obvious how the border guards are dismounting from the cabin of the 'technical' vehicle and running toward the island. The figure of a running man in dark clothing – this is Babansky – can be seen on the left. Kovalev, the driver of the APC, is standing on the roof of the vehicle and calling out to the soldiers to hurry to help Strelnikov. The second photo captures the moment when Bubenin's APC completed its raid into the rear area of the Chinese ambush and moved toward the Soviet riverbank. It is quite obvious how Strelnikov's command GAZ and Babansky's vehicle are burning (the tarpaulin on Strelnikov's GAZ has already completely burned).

The photographs look as though they were taken from a distance of no more than 100 metres. However, even a quick glance at a terrain map is enough to understand that there was a minimum of several hundred metres between the photographer and the border guards' vehicles. This means that the photographer used a special telephoto lens, which made the subject of the photo seem closer. Obviously, this had to have been planned in advance.

So here us what is strange: how could the Chinese filmmakers have missed that most important moment, when 'the Soviets were the first to open fire'? After all, in this case the remaining footage was no longer needed: see how we were attacked and we were forced to push them back and 'counterattack in self-defence'! Can you imagine how such a winning propaganda campaign could have succeeded? In this case, the world's public opinion would have unanimously been on Chairman Mao's side.

But you will not find any such footage. And a brilliant propaganda campaign for some reason did not take place. Why?

The answer is obvious: because it was the Chinese who were the first to open fire. That being said, the Chinese could not help but photograph who shot first, inasmuch as the cameramen were sent to the location of the events exclusively for a documented record of what took place. Everything was photographed and examined by whoever needed to do so, but we still are not meant to have access to these images. We still do not know who did the filming and whether or not this person is alive now. We also do not know who of the Chinese leadership had access to the secret. And, finally, we do not know whether these images have been kept. Nevertheless, there is a chance, and who knows, perhaps we will be witnesses to the final collapse of another myth about this conflict.

Chinese propaganda is still operating according to the patterns of the 'cultural revolution.' The following is a characteristic example.

The authors of this book have at their disposal several photographs taken these days on formerly Soviet Damansky Island (they can be found on the internet). The Chinese have a museum there, and a characteristic scene is depicted in one of the photos: a group of elderly tourists are listening to an explanation by a guide dressed in a military uniform. The faces of these people should be seen: the visitors are amazed and enthralled; the guide is smiling and condescending. One can imagine how the guide is describing the 'exploits' of the PLA soldiers in March 1969. In another photo a throng of Chinese pioneers with red neckties are catching the guide's every word as he talks about the heroism of their grandfathers. And as visual material there is a photo on display of a dead Soviet officer with a rather peculiar inscription: 'Senior Lieutenant Ivan, Chief of the Nizhne-Mikhaylovka Outpost, killed by us.' That is, the education process is exactly as it was in 1969. It seems that in the China of today they feel no remorse for what was done.

8
MANUSCRIPTS DO NOT BURN[1]

A.D. Konstantinov, former chief of the political department of the Iman Border Detachment, related this curious account to one of the authors. It turns out that several days after the first confrontation on Damansky Island he distributed to the border guards thin student notebooks and asked them to write down in them everything that they had seen with their own eyes during the battle. The idea was to

Veterans of the 2 March 1969 battle on Damansky Island (from left to right): Yu. Kozus, P. Kovalev, A. Bikuzin, V. Vishnevsky, V. Razmakhnin, Yu. Babansky. (Military Museum of Hanoi, via Albert Grandolini)

try in this way to recreate in detail a picture of the 2 March events. At that time this information was of great practical importance; now it is invaluable material for anyone researching the Damansky tragedy.

The border guards willingly wrote down their observations, and Konstantinov put the pile of notebooks on his work table. Sometime later he was summoned to a meeting in Moscow. When he returned, Aleksandr Dmitriyevich did not find the notebooks where he had left them, and subsequent searches led to nothing. It was clear that one of the officers was interested in the border guards' accounts and could not resist the temptation of – let us say in contemporary slang – 'privatising' the handwritten texts. Anyway, Konstantinov did not find the missing notebooks and was very sorry about this. He still told one of the authors that he had some suspicion as to the identity of the 'kidnapper'; however, there was no one to turn to, as that man was no longer alive. This conversation took place in summer 2000 at the Central Border Museum of the FSB RF, where Konstantinov worked as deputy chief of the museum for personnel and education.

Nine years passed and this old tale of the notebooks unexpectedly reintroduced itself. The fact is that in 2009 General I.I. Petrov's book *The Sino-Soviet Wars. The Truth about Damansky* was published, in which the following lines can be found:

> I accepted General Major A.N. Anikushin's post of chief of the political department of Pacific Ocean Border District. In addition to other positive qualities, this man sought to document events that he witnessed. I was convinced of this once again when, sometime later, I began to sort through the drawers of his work table. In one of them my attention was turned to a pile of notebooks. These were notes by those who took part in the battles on the Ussuri on 2 March 1969.[2]

Further on, Petrov states that he had clearly not found all the notebooks, inasmuch as only one of them (Private V. Razmakhnin's) belonged to a border guard from the Nizhne-Mikhaykovka outpost, while the remaining 10 notebooks contained entries from soldiers from the Kulebyakiny Sopki Outpost.

Razmakhnin's testimony about the shooting on Damansky was already cited above. Let us continue his account further:

> After the first burst I immediately lay down and loaded my machine gun, after which I sent a burst against the provocateurs, after which I began to shoot in short bursts and conserve my rounds, because we had two magazines (25 rounds in each) each. It was clear that the provocateurs had begun to fall; I don't know if I or someone else had hit them. From the adjoining riverbank they began to fire from machine guns and mortars along the island. To the side I saw some men in white camouflage smocks. I thought that they were ours, from Kulebyakiny Sopki, and I continued to fire against the provocateurs. A junior sergeant from tech support (I don't know his name) was next to me. Under heavy fire I began to crawl back closer to the riverbank. Here I caught sight of Privates Vishnevsky and Bikuzin, and in front were two soldiers from tech support. At this time the provocateurs started coming toward us. There and then I heard the noise of an armoured personnel carrier. The provocateurs opened heavy fire against it. Junior Sergeant Babansky ordered us to take up the defence. I occupied a position behind a tree and began to observe beyond the riverbank. At this time the provocateurs began to carry off the wounded, while fire intensified from the riverbank against the armoured personnel carrier. When the APC passed us, Junior Sergeant Babansky sent Private Yeremin to a power source to report to the outpost that we had no more rounds. He set off in the direction of the power source, not bending down, and then the junior sergeant shouted out to him. He turned toward Babansky, not understanding what the latter wanted from him. Babansky explained to Yeremin how he had to get to a power source, and the latter ran off. Having waited some time, we began to crawl toward the riverbank, in a line, covering one another. When I reached the riverbank I did not see Babansky and asked Private Bikuzin about him. It was about two o'clock in the afternoon. The sergeant from tech support asked "What do we do?" I said that we had to send up a flare and crawl into the bushes. Not far from the bushes

> I saw Babansky and Kozus. They were shooting. Then everyone gathered together and decided to signal the outpost using flares. I took off my flare gun and gave it to Jun. Sgt. Babansky. I don't know which flare he loaded, and I said that we would sneak out. Having jumped out from the bushes, we saw Lieutenant Colonel Konstantinov with men. After this we began to carry out our wounded and dead. That's all I know.

As is known, the decisive episode of the battle was the destruction of the command post for the Chinese ambush. Sergeant Pavel Sikushenko tells about this flank strike against the Chinese:

> When we drove up to the island we set off along it, downstream, covering several hundred metres. We wanted to get to the island itself, but we were not successful because nearly all of the vehicle's wheel assemblies had been pierced by bullets. After unsuccessful attempts to make it to the island, we drove on further. Having circled the island, we saw a bare patch of land, and the senior lieutenant ordered us to move along it. After we had gone deep into the channel, we began to see the figures of the provocateurs in the bushes, and we opened fire against them. The senior lieutenant fired at them with a machine gun, and we fired with automatic weapons through the embrasures. It was already difficult for us to move further along the channel, and the chief of the outpost order us to turn back.

Junior Sergeant V. Kanygin attests to the following:

> Puzyrev and I took cover behind trees and fired from the flank at the attacking provocateurs. As I later found out, our armoured personnel carrier had arrived in the provocateurs' flank and struck using a heavy machine gun, which decided the outcome of the battle. The provocateurs, having heard the shooting on the flank, began to gather their dead and wounded. Our rounds were running low. I didn't know what the provocateurs would subsequently attempt. Private Puzyrev gave me his rounds, leaving himself only four for whatever happened. I sent him for magazines, thinking that the reserve had arrived and had brought us rounds; after all, more than an hour had passed since the battle began. At this time the provocateurs had hastily withdrawn to their riverbank. Sometime later Puzyrev crawled up behind me and I crawled off to the riverbank. By this time the battle was over.

Private N. Puzyrev writes about Kanygin's actions:

> I saw that Junior Sergeant Kanygin was running not far to my right, and as soon as he reached the oaks that had grown together... he dropped down. I dropped to his left into the grass. He shouted at me: "Crawl to me." I was 8–10 metres away from him. As I crawled to him he was already firing bursts, separating two rounds from the next two rounds. The two of us began to fire in short bursts at the attackers, who were standing or kneeling. Kanygin told me to crawl to this oak tree and conserve the rounds. Talking with one another, we began to fire single shots, kneeling and trying to get as close as possible. The provocateurs tried to attack about four times, while at the same time, under the cover of their own men, they dragged off their dead and wounded. Four provocateurs ran out from the ambush without camouflage smocks. They dragged the wounded and dead along a single path. The provocateurs were shouting very loudly and were in a panic. There were 30–35 men here.

Having set off for ammunition, Puzyrev stumbled upon wounded Private Aniper. The two of them walked to the riverbank, when they caught sight of Bubenin's APC, which was returning after the flank attack on the Chinese ambush. Puzyrev relates how the APC had been knocked out of commission:

> APC No. 04 approached and covered us. Sergeant Sikushenko and Private Prosvirin jumped out of the side hatch to help protect the wounded. The hatch closed on its own. At this time a shell struck the APC. Shouts could be heard in it, and we began to drag men out of it: Junior Sergeant Larichkin, Private Putilov, Senior Lieutenant Bubenin, and others. The APC was full of smoke, and someone shouted: "Get Yermalyuk out." Another shell fell about two metres from the APC. The senior lieutenant said: "Move the wounded towards the island." Those who were not seriously wounded walked on their own to the riverbank.

Sergeant Pavel Sikushenko talks about this as well:

> When we drove up to the wounded we first covered them with armour, then I jumped into the side hatch to help the wounded. It was Aniper. Puzyrev and I had just managed to seat him inside the APC when I saw that our APC was somewhat shaking; after this we heard an explosion, and there was screaming there that made my blood run cold. After this we heard a whistle, and a second shell hit the turret. Then, a few minutes later, we heard a third shell.

Other border guards describe how an alarm was raised and how they arrived at Damansky, how they entered the battle and removed the wounded and dead from the battlefield. In some places there are some small discrepancies in these testimonies, which is completely natural, if we take into consideration the unexpectedness of what happened and the general stress of battle. The style of the accounts is noteworthy: all the soldiers write calmly, without particular emotion, as if they were only observers of it all, and not direct participants in the bloodshed. They report about their actions professionally – 'fired', 'crawled', 'saw', etc. Judging by everything, the soldiers understood how important their testimony was and, therefore, tried to present only the essence of the matter.

Many years after the events of 2 March 1969, Arkady Vasilyevich Shamov, the driver of Bubenin's APC, describes in a letter to the authors what he saw with his own eyes:

> In winter, when the ice had frozen on the river, we were sent on an APC to do our service by reinforcing the border. I served at the Kulebyakiny Sopki Outpost, where the outpost chief was Senior Lieutenant Bubenin.
>
> On the morning of 2 March I drove down to the river to bring back a barrel of water for the outpost, but a few minutes later a border guard ran up to me and said that I should quickly go to the outpost because the border was being violated. When I drove back to the outpost all personnel were already standing in combat readiness. They got into the APC and we drove to Damansky Island.
>
> When we reached the island I saw that all the vehicles had been put out of commission: the GAZ-69 and GAZ-63. Only the APC driven by P. Kovalev was not out of commission; Litvinov, the driver of Strelnikov's GAZ-69, was with him in the APC. I tried to drive onto the island, but couldn't, because the bank of the island was steep. Then all personnel dismounted onto the

island and accepted battle. At this time Kovalev's APC drove up to me. Artillery and grenade launchers were pounding us by direct laying. I also took a machine gun and ran to the island, but I recall that the vehicle couldn't be left behind. I climbed into the APC, loaded the machine gun, and began to cruise along the island. Several border guards, headed by Bubenin, came up to me from the island. They came into my APC.

I left from the north and moved a distance of 40 metres along the island. I saw the Chinese, but I thought that they had not seen me because I was moving behind them. Bubenin fired from the machine guns. I pulled close to the island; there were Chinese there, 10–12 men. When I drove closer to the Chinese, I ran over two or three of them. At this time the wheel assemblies of the APC were all broken, and only two wheels were undamaged. Then a shell from a grenade launcher fell onto the turret. Bubenin was seriously wounded, but I, with difficulty, drove the vehicle out of the zone where the Chinese were pounding us, from the island and from the Chinese riverbank. I drove across the island, reached a secret power source, and phoned the duty officer. He asked where Bubenin was, and I answered that he was seriously wounded. Bubenin quickly came up and began to talk with the duty officer. Kovalev's APC arrived, and Bubenin boarded it and went into battle from the south side of the island. I took a machine gun and Petrov[3] and I began to shoot the Chinese, who were withdrawing from the island. The battle quickly ended; a helicopter arrived with Chief of the Political Department Konstantinov.

9
GENERAL SHCHUR'S PAINFUL MEMORIES

The battle on the border with China came out of the blue for the Soviet leadership. No one had ever imagined that an ideological altercation with the Chinese could lead to an exchange of shots and bloodshed. But this had happened, and it was necessary to investigate the events and reach some conclusions. As was customary in such cases, a State Commission was convened, and General Major Vasily Timofeyevich Shchur was made a member of the Commission.

V.T. Shchur was born in Kanev (Cherkasy *Oblast* in Ukraine) in 1918. Before serving in the Army, he had studied in a train repair factory at a school of factory apprenticeship in Kiev. After that, he worked as a foreman and an inspector of a technical control department. In 1938 he volunteered to serve with the border troops – serving in the Far East, Ukraine, Turkestan, and Georgia, and occupying various political positions. In 1969 he was deputy chief of the Political Directorate of the KGB's Main Directorate of Border

Members of the State Commission, Command of the Pacific Ocean Border District, relatives and friends of I. Strelnikov. Sitting: General Major V.T. Shchur (first on the left), Lidia Strelnikova with her son (centre), General Colonel N.S. Zakharov (second from the right) and General Major V.F. Lobanov (first on the right). Standing: General Lieutenant V.A. Matrosov (first on the left), Colonel D.V. Leonov (centre) and General Major A.N. Anikushin (first on the right). (from V.N. Volik)

Troops, under the USSR Council of Ministers. At different times Shchur was awarded the Order of Lenin, Order of the Red Star, the Order of the Patriotic War, first and second class, and other medals. At the end of his long and eventful life, Shchur put pen to paper and wrote his memoirs to pass on his experiences to future generations of border guards and to anyone interested in his country's history. By all accounts, the Damansky events were one of the most significant and tragic pages of his life journey.

Shchur wrote the following about how he became aware of the battle on Damansky:[1]

> On the night of 2 March, the duty officer at the KGB's Main Directorate of Border Troops telephoned me and relayed to me the order from General Colonel Pavel Ivanovich Zyryanov, chief of the border troops, to go to the directorate in full field uniform, which the latter had received from Chairman of the KGB Yu.V. Andropov.
>
> First Deputy Chief of the KGB, General Colonel Nikolay Stepanovich Zakharov, and Chief of Staff of the Border Troops, General Lieutenant Vadim Alexandrovich Matrosov, were already there. We entered the Chairman's office somewhat agitated. In the presence of P.I. Zyryanov, we were given concise information about the events on Damansky Island. In this regard Yu.V. Andropov said: "Not everything is clear to me. The detachment's command is with all its subunits on some Soviet Army exercises. The detachment duty officer does not know the exact situation, he reports everything hypothetically, imprecisely and unclearly. Therefore, Generals Zakharov, Matrosov and Shchur must fly immediately from Vnukovo Airport to the 57th Detachment. There you should investigate in place everything that has happened. Bring back the command and all subunits from the exercises; ascertain the grouping of the Chinese provocateurs; and help the detachment. Leonid Ilich Brezhnev just told me that it is necessary to take all measures to extinguish this armed conflict, and not allow Mao's criminal group to draw our country into a major war."
>
> Lieutenant Colonel Petr Alexandrovich Ivanchishin, deputy chief of the Political Directorate, and I sped in a car to Vnukovo Airport without paying attention to any road signs.

At the airfield in Iman (today Dalnerechensk), General Major Vasily Fedorovich Lobanov, chief of troops of the Pacific Ocean Border District and Colonel Demokrat Vladimirovich Leonov, chief of the 57th Border Detachment, met the Moscow commission. Several minutes later, they all flew by helicopter to the Nizhne-Mikhaylovka Outpost.

Having arrived, the Commission began to investigate the circumstances of the military clash. It was not easy – many participants of the battle had already been transported to the hospital, and some of the soldiers were in state of depression caused by the sudden deaths of their friends and brothers-in-arms:

> We flew in a helicopter over Damansky Island and looked at the adjacent Chinese territory up to the Hunzy border post. It was obvious that the Chinese had not recovered, as the post was in confusion; the men were running around, and some of them were shooting at our helicopter.
>
> We landed and studied the terrain, the location where Strelnikov had perished. Upon our return to the outpost we obtained more specific information from soldiers and officers. After that it became clear where and how the border troops of the 1st and 2nd outposts courageously fought against the enemy, who outnumbered them by a factor of ten.
>
> We could visualise Chief of the 1st Outpost Vitaly Bubenin's actions and Junior Sergeant Babansky's courageous deed. Instantly, we three generals decided to recommend them for the Hero of the Soviet Union award. Following Zakharov's order, I wrote a short report right there at the outpost.
>
> Upon our return to the detachment, we visited the hospital to meet and talk with V. Bubenin and other wounded men, but to no avail: Bubenin was covered in bandages from the head down, only his eyes were visible, and he was deaf due to a concussion. He was extremely pleased with our visit.

Gennady Serebrov in the hospital. (from V.N. Volik)

In addition to the visit to the hospital, the members of the commission considered it their duty to view the corpses of the men who had died, who had been laid in the barn at the Nizhne-Mikhaylovka Outpost. According to Shchur's description, a minor event took place here associated with Private Gennady Serebrov, whose testimony was cited earlier when describing the deaths of Rabovich's group at the beginning of the 2 March battle.

Serebrov had been wounded and had lost consciousness. One of the Chinese had gone up to him and struck the wounded guard with an SKS bayonet. Apparently satisfied that the Soviet soldier was dead, the Chinese soldier withdrew. After the battle Serebrov, still unconscious, was transported to the Nizhne-Mikhaylovka Outpost and put in the barn with all the dead border guards. General Shchur describes what happened next:

> I cannot say by what power or what prompted me to take the pulse of each of the dead men. I began to feel for the pulse of those lying in the row, one after the other, and when I reached the twelfth "dead" border guard, I had a vague feeling that there was life in this body. I quickly asked for a mirror and a sheepskin coat. There was no mirror to be found at the outpost, so I asked Lidia Strelnikova, who was still waiting for the return of her living husband, Ivan, for one.
>
> Having heated and wiped the mirror with a cloth so that the surface was dry, I covered the "dead" man with the coat, and a few minutes later I found barely noticeable spots of moisture on the surface of the mirror. We immediately moved the wounded man

to the kitchen, covered him with a sheepskin coat and fur coats, and lit the stove. After some time, the beat of his pulse could be felt ever so slowly. His body gradually got warmer. By evening we had sent him to the hospital. Unfortunately, under those circumstances I was unable to keep track of his name, and to this day I do not know whom I saved from death.

Private Serebrov was the only Soviet witness of the beginning of the clash to survive from both Strelnikov's and Rabovich's groups. The Chinese tried to kill every witness so no Soviet soldier could tell the truth about what really happened on the morning of 2 March. Only Serebrov was able to give details about how the border troops were attacked by the Chinese. His story eased the work of the Soviet Commission, whose job it was to try and clarify all the circumstances surrounding the incident.

As to this part of Shchur's memoirs, there are serious doubts that it was only he who found and saved Serebrov. The State Commission had arrived at the battlefield on 3 March, only a day after the clash. All the fallen had been placed in the barn and temperatures were below freezing, so it was highly unlikely that Serebrov would have still been alive when Shchur appeared at the outpost. It seems Serebrov was saved by someone else. The story was also recounted by A.D. Konstantinov, former chief of the political department of Iman Border Guards, but he does not mention who saved Serebrov.

At that time, as the members of the commission studied the situation, the 1st and 2nd Border Outposts prepared their farewells.

Warrant Officer V. Pashintsev and several assistants carried the dead to a heated bathhouse, where they warmed up the bodies, washed them, dressed them in clean uniforms, and placed them in coffins, and then once again returned to their cold quarters.

On 5 March the parents and loved ones of the dead men began to arrive at the Nizhne-Mikhaylovka Outpost. The difficult mission of meeting and finding accommodations for them fell on the shoulders of G.M. Zhestkov, assistant chief of the Iman Border Detachment's political department for Komsomol work. The officer had to listen to a lot from the upset, heartbroken people. As Zhestkov himself recalls today, only after the funeral, when, according to Russian tradition, they sat and remembered the dead, did a feeling of unity in their perceived misfortune arise among all who were present.

On 6 March 1969 the funeral for the dead guards took place at the outposts No. 1 (Kulebyakiny Sopki) and No. 2 (Nizhne-Mikhaylovka). General Zakharov ordered V. Matrosov to go to outpost No. 1 to organise the mourning. Shchur was ordered to do the same at post No. 2.

General Shchur recalls:

> The mass grave, warmed up from frozen soil, was slowly dug. At the outpost there were only a crowbar, two axes, and a fire hook available that were appropriate for the work. With great difficulty the inhabitants of Nizhne-Mikhaylovka procured a pneumatic hammer, and, using this, a mass grave was dug for the burial of the 20 men. Each grave was marked with a hastily made board and a cross.

In a letter to one of the authors, N.I. Popov corroborates the same thing:

> They began to dig the common grave at the 2nd outpost with crowbars and picks, but the ground was very frozen. Then they brought a compressor from Luchegorsk; however, all the same, progress was very slow. Then, at night, while the border guards were resting and no one was in the outpost's yard, the combat engineers laid explosives (that being said, they miscalculated the power of the charge) and there was a detonation. Clods of earth flew in all directions, and some glass in the barracks was shattered. Someone shouted that the Chinese were firing on the outpost; everyone ran to the strong point...
>
> The tractor was of great help with the digging, shovelling out the earth. By 6 March the grave for the 20 dead border guards from the 2nd Outpost had been dug out.

The morning meeting at the Nizhne-Mikhaylovka Outpost was opened by Colonel D.V. Leonov, who said a few words about what had happened and about the heroic behaviour of the fallen soldiers.

Relatives of the dead soldiers arrive at the funeral. (from V.N. Volik)

6 March 1969, Nizhne-Mikhaylovka Outpost. Colonel D. Leonov gives a speech. To his right, from left to right, are Generals N.S. Zakharov, V.T. Shchur, and V.F. Lobanov. (from V.N. Volik)

7 March 1969, Iman. Lidia Strelnikova with her son at her husband's grave. (from V.N. Volik)

General Colonel N.S. Zakharov said the following:

> We are accompanying on their final journey the hero border guards who died in battle against violators of the Soviet border, who treacherously attacked our soldiers by surprise on orders from the Chinese authorities. The treacherous incursion into Soviet territory on 2 March was not a chance occurrence. From the time that the PRC leadership began to conduct a risky policy of exacerbating Sino-Soviet relations, provocations on the border and arrogant claims to Soviet territory have intensified. The provocation on Damansky Island on the Ussuri River was especially insidious and brazen. The Soviet border guards suffered casualties, but did not waver. They boldly entered battle and drove the provocateurs from Soviet territory. And it will be so in the future, if the flagrant Chinese nationalists try to violate the sacred borders of the great Soviet Motherland.[2]

Later, V. Grinko, P. Kravchenko, V. Krasnov, A. Bartovskaya and other representatives of the Primorsky *Krai* community spoke. They talked about the exploits of the dead men and about the continuation of military traditions of the older generation and denounced the dishonour of the Maoist provocateurs. Yu. Babansky and V. Kanygin, who had truly displayed heroism in the 2 March battle, spoke on behalf of those who had taken part in the battle. Some of those who participated in the funeral recalled that Babansky demonstrated a tact that was surprising for his young age, calming in every way possible the parents of the dead soldiers. He spent an especially long time with the parents of Nikolay Dergach, whom he had known well before their military service.

Parting with the dead is always sad, but in this case the painful loss was especially hard, since the dead men were very young soldiers who had perished in peacetime. This circumstance shaped the general picture of how the day of 6 March 1969 progressed at the two outposts of the Iman Border Detachment. General Shchur recalls this most sorrowful moment for him:

> As the coffins were lowered into the graves, there was a horrible scream. Many of the victims' relatives jumped into the trench after the coffins. We had to create a group of several men to literally carry those people out.
>
> When the funeral was over, I stood next to Zakharov. An elderly woman came up, took me by the lapels of my overcoat, and screamed: "You, monster, you killed my only son!" Then she fell to the ground, having torn off my overcoat. She was immediately carried to the barracks, where doctors left her, but she was unable to walk without assistance. I didn't hold back my tears, and Zakharov began to calm me down.

On this day nine border guards were buried at the Kulebyakiny Sopki Outpost. A day later officers I. Strelnikov and N. Buinevich were put into the ground. They were buried in the centre of Iman.

Most of the dead border guards were buried at the outposts, although many relatives asked to take the dead bodies back home. V. Shchur wrote the following about the man who made the decision:

> We appealed to Yu.V. Andropov, and he appealed to Brezhnev. For three days our commission negotiated with Brezhnev personally about the burial place for the dead soldiers. As a result, the 'strongest' won: Leonid Ilich was unrelenting – he ordered the deceased to be buried only in Nizhne-Mikhaylovka. The reason was so as not to agitate the whole country by spreading a wave of indignation... Brezhnev allowed only two officers, Ivan Strelnikov and Nikolay Buinevich, to be buried in Iman.
>
> After the burial there was an organised commemoration in the rooms of the local cultural centre. Initially there was silence. I spoke first and then gave the floor to General Zakharov. His spoke well and meaningfully. Only after two glasses of alcohol did I feel warmth in conversations with the relatives.

During the wake, an episode took place that had consequences. The story is not so flattering, but what happened, happened:

> Zakharov's speech was heartfelt, but at the end he made a mistake, because he promised that every year two members of every family would be able to visit their sons' graves, and that all their expenses would be paid by the KGB. It seems that he had not coordinated this idea at the top, but the first year it happened just as he said. However, in following years, problems arose, and we, in the Main Directorate of the Border Troops and in the Political Directorate, felt this mistake for a long time. Moreover, Zakharov himself had retired few years later. As I later found out, the main opponents to Zakharov's promise were General Colonel Tsvigun, first deputy chairman of the KGB, and General Malygin, deputy chairman for materiel and technical procurement, who had come to the KGB from the administrative department of the CC CPSU.

However difficult the mourning events may have been, the members of the commission did not forget for one minute the main reason they had come to the Far East: to study the circumstances of what had happened and to take measures to increase the combat readiness of the border guards. First and foremost, the commission began to look for the guilty parties responsible for the death of 32 soldiers and officers as a result of the surprise attack. Judging from General Shchur's memoirs, the members of the commission did not look for a scapegoat but tried to objectively assess the actions of all officers involved.

The command of the 57th Border Detachment (Colonel D. Leonov was the chief) was blamed for poor collection and analysis of information about the situation at the border, especially those areas disputed by the Chinese. The organisation of joint exercises with Soviet Army subunits was found to be inadequate, because it was not possible for Leonov to efficiently receive reports about what was happening on the border. It was also said that there was an absence of reliable communication between Leonov and detachment headquarters, and that there were unclear orders from the detachment duty officer.

> Apparently, at this time General Colonel Zakharov decided to relieve Colonel D. Leonov from his post. He had not consulted with Matrosov and me, and on returning to Moscow he said this in a report to Yu.V. Andropov. The latter asked: "What is the opinion of the main directorate of the border troops and the political directorate?" We did not expect this, and both of us objected to such a step during such a difficult time for the detachment; moreover, we knew of Leonov's capabilities from working together in Georgia. Andropov said, "You see, if the command objects, we will not do it."
>
> As for the chief of the political directorate of the border district, we dismissed him shortly after. He was ill, hardly working, dozing off all the time at work, and he felt bad, his work was mediocre. I knew him when we worked together in the 1950s in the political department of the Turkmen District. He was active, hard-working, and a professionally trained officer. Therefore, seeing him in the 57th Detachment during the events on Damansky Island, I frankly pitied him. But work is work, especially the border service, and there is no room for laziness and indifference.

Historians who studied the clash on Damansky and the Soviet veterans of the battle spoke and wrote much about the role played by General Colonel O.A. Losik, commander of the Far Eastern Military District. The general opinion was that Losik was indecisive in his actions to repel the Chinese attack, resulting in avoidable casualties.

After the conflict ended he was recalled to Moscow and appointed Chief of the Armoured Troops Academy, named for R.Ya. Malinovsky. From this arises the natural question: was this a promotion or a demotion? On the one hand, in the military environment, leaving command work for teaching was always considered an honourable exile. On the other hand, Losik's new post was in Moscow, the capital of the country, under the watch of the top leadership of the USSR. In addition, in 1975 he was promoted to the rank of Marshal of Armoured Troops.

Only now, reading General V. Shchur's memoirs, can one really assess Losik's behaviour during the events on the Ussuri River:

The last minutes… (from V.N. Volik)

After the burial... the three of us drove to the headquarters of the Far Eastern Military District (in Khabarovsk) for a talk with the commander of the troops, General Colonel Losik. After updating him on the battle on Damansky Island, we politely, but firmly expressed our opinion that the border guards had fought against the Chinese on their own. We asked him: how can such passivity on the part of the Soviet Army units and subunits, particularly the 135th Motorised Rifle Division, be explained, when, according to the plan of cooperation with the 57th Border Detachment, it was supposed to cover the Iman axis and, if any battle situation developed on the Sino-Soviet border, to help the border troops? Why did the district command, in our opinion, adopt the attitude of an outside observer regarding the events on Damansky? Why, having information about the concentration of Chinese military formations near the state border, did the command not take any reinforcement measures, even if only symbolic gestures, which might have dissuaded the Chinese from instigating an armed conflict? We asked a number of other questions as well.

On being asked such questions, General Colonel Losik became nervous and began to silently pace up and down his office; after a short pause, he gave the following answer:

"I was appointed here by the country's highest leadership not to react immediately to any petty border conflicts, even armed ones. I rely on the border guards to resolve them independently, with their own forces. In this situation, the units and formations that I command acted correctly. As the district commander, I have no claims on the commander of the 135th Motor-Rifle Division, which covers this strategic axis. I did not receive any instructions from the General Staff or the Minister of Defence on this matter, even though they knew about the armed conflict on the border. Why didn't the command of the border troops, in the person of General Colonel Zyryanov, or KGB Chairman Andropov appeal to the Minister of Defence and the General Staff for support for the Border Troops? Therefore, we do not see that we were guilty here. I alone cannot take overall responsibility for the fate of our country in cases of serious armed conflicts."

Following his responses to our questions, it became clear to us that he had not assessed the events that had taken place, nor had he taken decisive measures to help the border troops, because of his indecision and fear of what might happen. General Colonel Zakharov rose from his chair (as did the rest of us) and stated:

"Comrade Military District Commander, I and my comrades are totally dissatisfied with your answers and explanations. After all, the fact is that 29 soldiers and 2 officers perished, and many wounded men are being treated in the hospital in Filino right now. All of them are young and devoted to our Motherland and to their military oath. The impression is that in this case you, as the commander, demonstrated indifference and indecision, if not worse, towards the fate of these men and interests of the state. We, and I in particular, as a first deputy chairman of the KGB, will report our general opinion to Yuri Vladimirovich Andropov, who is waiting for our conclusions, and I will ask him to discuss the issue in the Politburo with the participation of Leonid Ilich Brezhnev. That is all that we can reply to your explanations."

On hearing this, Losik asked us to soften our conclusions and not to report the findings in this context to Andropov. He said, we will draw our conclusions from the bloody events and discuss them at the district Military Council and will not allow such things to happen again. He said goodbye to us, and we left the Far Eastern Military District headquarters with the firm intention to report the contents of the conversation to Chairman of the KGB Yu.V. Andropov. And we did so on our return to Moscow.

I know that there was a harsh talk in Moscow with the commander of the Far Eastern Military District. During the second Chinese provocation on 15 March 1969, 135th Division units and subunits behaved more dynamically, but not resolutely enough until the last moment. This resulted in the death of Colonel Demokrat Vladimirovich Leonov, chief of the 57th Border Detachment, who, seeing the critical situation Yanshin's manoeuvre group was in and unable to request fire and tank support for them, took over command of the tank himself and tried to help his border guards. But he was wounded and eventually died.

Obviously, Losik's actions during the conflict on Damansky were assessed negatively by the country's leadership. It was the reason why the general was dismissed from the post of military district commander and appointed as chief of a military academy. As for Moscow and the promotion to the rank of marshal, this can clearly be seen as the personnel policies of Brezhnev and his entourage: do not offend renowned people. After all, Losik had fought in the war against Finland in 1939–40, was a veteran of the Great Patriotic War, and had been awarded the title of Hero of the Soviet Union in 1944. Considerations of elementary fairness possibly also played a role: it was not only Losik who was responsible for the defence of the Soviet Far East. The Ministry of Defence and the General Staff were also responsible. However, the Moscow generals preferred not to assume any responsibility for the battle on the border, instead placing the blame on the Far Eastern Military District command. In general, they underperformed. At least the officers and soldiers of the border guards and Soviet Army servicemen who fought on Damansky were not thinking about any responsibility, but, risking their lives, fought against the enemy.

In a letter to one of the authors, N.I. Popov, a veteran of the border fighting, described General V.T. Shchur as follows:

> I had met him several times. Both when he came to our detachment as a member of the State Commission at the time of the Damansky events, and later, in Moscow, where I was studying in the Higher Border Improvement Courses. He was a strong-willed, intelligent officer. It was interesting to listen to his talks and adopt them.

Vasily Timofeyevich Shchur passed away in September 2011, leaving behind books and fond memories.

10
EVENTS ON THE BORDER THROUGH WESTERN EYES

The events on the Sino-Soviet border were attentively followed in all countries throughout the world, inasmuch as a border conflict between two such great powers could have negative repercussions on the fate of any nation.

In particularly dangerous situations, the politicians always have the last word, and diplomats and the military are obligated to carry out their will. However, in order that politicians make no mistakes and make the correct decisions, they must understand well what has happened – it is here that professional intelligence officers and scholars come to their aid. For reasons that can be understood, we do not know much about the former; however, the work of the latter is often available to the public and the results of their research become the subject of discussion not only among specialists. It was just in this way that information about the events on Damansky reached Western readers.

In the works that were written by European and American scholars about the Sino-Soviet Border War, one constantly encounters very similar phrases. This means that there was someone who studied the events in sufficient detail, thereby giving impetus to further research. It is very simple to understand all this. After all, many authors of scholarly works are traditionally very meticulous when citing each other; therefore, one can immediately arrive at the primary source of the materials being used. Judging by everything, the earliest and most important research on this theme was that of American professor Thomas Robinson, which was published in August 1970.[1]

Robinson's work was done with the support of the US Air Force command. As was written on the title page, 'Views or conclusions contained in this study should not be interpreted as representing the official opinion or policy of the United States Air Force.'

Chapter 3 of Robinson's work begins with a description of the Damansky Region; for the first time the precise coordinates of the island are pointed out – 133° 51' E longitude and 46° 51' N latitude, which is approximately correct. The distance from Khabarovsk is also given – around 180 miles (about 290 kilometres) southwest of the town. Two nearby settlements are named: Nizhne-Mikhaylovka (5 miles to the south) and Hunzy (directly south of the island). Further on, the author mentions the Chinese claims to Damansky because of its proximity to the Chinese riverbank, which is manifested especially clearly when the Ussuri River becomes shallow. Robinson writes the following about the island:

> The island itself is, by testimony of both sides, uninhabited, although Chinese fishermen apparently use it for drying their nets, and both nationalities may do some logging on it...
>
> The water level of the Ussuri varies over thirty feet, and during the short but rainy summer flash floods are not uncommon. The characteristics of the immediate area are similar to those all along the Ussuri: boggy marshes along both sides, low elevation but slightly higher on the Chinese side, sparse population along the river front, and inhospitability to agriculture...
>
> The island is wooded for the most part, although there are some open areas, and the elevation rises in places to as much as 20 feet above the water's edge. [pp.34–35]

Robinson uses Soviet sources in his work, for the most part, therefore, he not only knows the location of the border outposts, but can also assess their tactical qualities:

> The Soviets maintain two border outposts in the area, one just south of the island, which until March 2 was commanded by Senior Lieutenant Ivan Ivanovich Strelnikov, and the other just to the north, commanded at the time by Senior Lieutenant Vitaliy Dmitriyevich Bubenin. The southern post has the disadvantage that its line of sight does not include the island itself (although the river-arm and the Chinese bank can be seen) and thus on-the-spot patrolling is necessary to determine Chinese presence on the island. The Chinese border post, named Kung-szu[2] after the local Chinese settlement, appears to be located on a hillock directly across from the island. Differing from the terrain in other sectors of the Ussuri boundary, there is extensive marshland on the Soviet, but not the Chinese, side of the river, in winter forcing vehicles to detour about two miles before they can move onto the ice toward the island. In March the river is frozen nearly solid, as it is possible to drive multi-ton vehicles over the ice, and the ice does not completely break up until nearly May. The average snow cover is only a few inches, meaning that frost penetrates several feet and delays the spring until late May. [p.35]

Robinson writes rather objectively about the 2 March events, without the excesses and myth-making those are so characteristic of many Russian authors. Of course, there is still some imprecision:

> What happened on 2 March? Unfortunately, only the participants were at the scene of battle and most of them are dead. Further, only the Soviets have given a detailed view of the events, gleaned

from testimony of survivors and from a special investigative team. Because almost no factual reports are available from the Chinese, our analysis is likely to be slanted toward the Soviet side. Despite these limitations, it is possible to reconstruct a composite account of what probably went on. [pp.35–36]

Indeed, after the March events a propaganda campaign was launched in China, relying not on facts, but rather on whipping up military hysteria. No PRC officials or Chinese journalists tried to oppose the Soviet announcements with any convincing factual material. Everything boiled down to invective and accusing the USSR of all mortal sins.

In his work Robinson does use publications from the Chinese press and Chinese radio broadcasts. It is another matter that he had more Soviet information.

On the night of March 1–2, about 300 Chinese troops (the Chinese say their defenders were a mixed group of frontier guards and regular PLA soldiers) dressed in white camouflage crossed the ice from the Chinese bank to Damansky Island, dug foxholes in a wooden area overlooking the southernmost extremity, laid telephone wire to the command post on the Chinese bank, and lay down for the night on straw mats.

Sometime early in the morning, the man on duty at Strelnikov's outpost south of the island noticed activity on the Chinese bank, which he reported to his superiors. Around 11:00 a.m., a group of 20 or 30 armed Chinese were seen to begin moving toward the island, shouting Maoist slogans as they came. [pp.36–37]

The number of Chinese in the group was established quite precisely: there were 30 of them – in no way only around 20. As for the slogans they were shouting, according to Soviet veterans there had been a meeting at the Chinese border post – naturally with shouts and waving of quotation books.

Seeing them, Strelnikov and an undetermined number of his subordinates climbed into two armored personnel carriers, a truck, and a command car, and set off for the southern extremity of the island to meet the Chinese. Arriving on the island (or perhaps remaining on the ice covering the river-arm to the west of the island) a few minutes later, Strelnikov and seven or eight others, including his deputy, Senior Lieutenant Buinevich, dismounted and moved out to warn the oncoming Chinese, as they had several times previously. Following a procedure developed for such occasions, the Russians strapped their automatic rifles to their chests (reports differ: some say they left their weapons behind).

The time was now about 11:15 a.m. The Russians linked arms to prevent the Chinese from passing. It is not clear whether any verbal exchange occurred, although the Chinese reports imply that an altercation took place. In any case, the Chinese arrayed themselves in rows and appeared to be unarmed. But when the Chinese had advanced to about 20 feet from the Russian group, the first row suddenly scattered to the side, exposing the second line of Chinese, who quickly pulled submachine guns from under their coats and opened fire on the Russian group. [p.37]

Nothing is known about the Soviet border guards linking arms. Apart from that, the dynamics of the events were different: it was not the Chinese who went to the border guards, but actually the Soviet soldiers who moved closer to the awaiting Chinese.

Further on Robinson describes the death of Rabovich's group:

Strelnikov and six of his companions were killed outright. Simultaneously, from an ambush to the Russian's right, the 300 Chinese in foxholes also opened fire, catching the entire Russian unit by surprise. Mortar, machine gun, and anti-tank gunfire also commenced at that moment (it was now between 11:17 and 11:20 a.m.) from the Chinese side. The Chinese apparently then charged the Soviets, and hand-to-hand fighting ensued. The Soviet unit was apparently overrun, and the Chinese (according to Soviet charges) took 19 prisoners and killed them on the spot. [p.37]

A mistake was made here: 19 men from both groups (Strelnikov's and Rabovich's) were killed. Akulov and Serebrov were not among them. And, of course, there were no prisoners.

[The Chinese] also carried away Soviet equipment, which they later put on display. Evidently the Russian survivors were able to fight back, however, now under the command of Junior Sergeant Yuri Babinski.[3]

Seeing the battle, Senior Lieutenant Bubenin and nearly his entire border post north of Damansky set out for the scene. [pp.37–38]

Regarding 'nearly his entire border post' there is a clear overstatement here: according to Bubenin himself, 22 border guards (that is, less than half) left with him on the APC.

Racing up in an armored car, [Bubenin] succeeded in gaining the right flank of the Chinese, forcing them to divide their fire. But he also found himself in the middle of the island and in the middle of the ambush that the Chinese had prepared for Strelnikov (the latter had not proceeded that far). Bubenin's vehicle was hit and disabled, and he himself was wounded and shell-shocked. He managed to get into another armored car and direct the battle from it. A series of melees ensued, with charges by both sides. Finally, the Russians state, they pinned down, for a time surrounded, and then forced the remaining 50 to 60 Chinese to retreat to their side of the bank. [p.38]

The Soviet press does not cite these numbers, although Robinson does cite the Russians. It is possible that some other information sources were used.

The Chinese took all their wounded with them, although they left behind some equipment. The entire battle lasted about two hours, and the Russians were so short-handed that civilians had to be pressed into service as ammunition bearers. [p.38]

This statement refers, apparently, to the Avdeyevs.[4] However, whereas Robinson's use of the English expression 'pressed into service' implies that these civilians were forcibly recruited, it should be clarified that no one 'forcibly recruited' the Avdeyevs to serve as ammunition bearers: they took the initiative for this themselves.

Some Russian authors also draw attention to the use of common village sleighs as a mode of transport for delivering ammunition. They explain this fact as being poor preparation for the conflict on the part of the border guards. The authors of such statements have made a mistake, inasmuch as the chosen method of delivering ammunition and weapons is actually completely appropriate for the natural and climatic conditions of the region of the military operations.

> Although both sides claimed victory, neither Russian nor Chinese forces remained permanently on the island after the battle was over, although the Soviets periodically moved off and on at will. [p.38]

There is an inaccuracy here: the Soviet border guards did not periodically visit Damansky, but rather continuously patrolled the island with reinforced details. This continued until the new, much more massive clash on 15 March.

The events of 2 March were reflected not only in Robinson's work, but also in the works of other authors and writing teams. The most notable of them is the multi-volume *History of China*, written by scholars at Cambridge University. Obviously, Robinson's standing as the leading Western specialist on the history of the Sino-Soviet Border War was generally recognised: it was he who was entrusted with that part of Volume 15 that covers the events on Damansky Island.[5]

An important part of Robinson's research was the search for an answer to the questions: Who needed an armed conflict on the border and why? Robinson discusses one of the possible reasons for the clash: 'local initiative':

> The first possibility is that either the Chinese or the Soviet local border force commander may have had much freedom of action. Standing orders from Peking or Moscow may have given local commanders enough latitude so that they might initiate military action if growing tension along the border seemed to warrant it. If this was the case, study of the outbreaks should focus on the chain of command from the political center through the military, the policies behind such orders, and the probable content of the orders, rather than on the competing cases for ownership of Damansky Island . . .
>
> We know from one source[6] that the Soviet border commanders had what would seem to be a great deal of latitude, delegated to them on the theory that in an emergency they would not have time to cable Moscow for instructions and the possibility that they would exceed their authority would be balanced by their having to answer to the center for all actions. [pp.41–42]

In the above-mentioned note, Robinson mentions that the USSR border units were a subunit of the KGB, and, therefore, their chiefs were not obliged to report about the events on the border to the command of the local army units. He also expresses some surprise about the fact that the border troops alone managed to secure victory over the more than 300 Chinese. This latter circumstance is, indeed surprising, but facts are facts: Bubenin's, Kanygin's, and Babansky's small and scattered groups did, in fact, succeed in defeating a much larger enemy.

> It is possible that Chinese border authorities had similar rights and duties, but in China the administrative situation is less clear. Regular border troops may have been supplemented by People's Liberation Army units and the Heilungkiang[7] Production and Construction Corps.
>
> Both sides allege that there had been previous incidents in the neighborhood of Damansky Island. If one or both of the local border commanders decided that unless he took action his patrol and construction operations would be so severely impaired as to threaten the safety of his men or the border security in his area, he would feel it his duty to stoutly draw the line at some geographical or psychological point . . .
>
> Another local possibility is that chance played a greater part than we have been led to believe by Soviet and Chinese sources. [p.43]

So, can the 2 March fighting by explained as the initiative of local chiefs or even chance? Of course not.

The fact is that procedures in the USSR and China were quite strict, and 'every cricket knew its own hearth'. It is difficult to imagine that some representative of the local authorities would be ready to take such responsibility on himself. The entire history of the Soviet Union and PRC teaches citizens of these countries one simple truth: in any situation it is better to keep a low profile and not stand out. As for a chance occurrence, the details of the 2 March battle clearly reject this (Robinson also rejects this idea a little later in his article).

Having dealt with 'local initiative' and 'chance', Robinson shifts to the internal politics of China's leaders:

> [It is possible] that the Chinese "Maoist" leadership perpetrated the March 2 incident as a means of diverting attention from tensions built up during the Cultural Revolution, and that it planned to use the resulting war scare as an incentive to carry through reforms that had run into popular opposition. Among the latter . . . were the permanent relocation of several tens of millions of urban residents to the countryside; reform of the medical system through the "barefoot doctors" campaign, which, although it extended rudimentary medical services to the lowest levels, also disrupted the medical system and temporarily lowered medical standards and impeded disease control; the reform of the educational system, to put production teams in charge of staffing and financing basic education (where the state had helped before); and the militarization of industry and education, by elevating "worker-peasant propaganda teams" to leadership positions and by installing military leadership and organization, ending hopes of putting the economy on a rational basis. In addition, the military dominated and then began to dissolve the "mass organizations," as the Red Guards and their revolutionary rebel allies were now called. [pp.50–51]

Speaking later about the influence of the army commanders, Robinson presents the hopes of many Chinese leaders: in case of problems on the border, the military would leave to pursue its immediate function and stop interfering in civilian administration issues. As for Mao and his entourage, they saw all threats to the policies of the 'cultural revolution', and in searching for a way out might choose a surprise action that no one expected. This is how Mao Zedong hoped to resolve a twofold problem: overcoming popular opposition and obtaining from the delegates of the upcoming meeting of the CPC *carte blanche* to carry out his policies. Did Mao understand, however, the riskiness of his ploy? Robinson answers as follows:

> The counter argument that the Soviets possessed superior force along the border and would overwhelm a Chinese attack was possibly met with the assertions that first the communist movement in China has faced such situations before and has won; second, that the Soviet Union is a "paper tiger" that would not retaliate in a manner that could not be handled at the border; and third, that such incidents could only be useful to China

> in teaching "by negative example" the nature of Soviet "social imperialism." [p.53]

Finally, the American scholar also sees foreign policy reasons for the Chinese leadership to have set forth into open conflict with the USSR. In his opinion, there are three such reasons:

> One explanation is that the Chinese political and military leadership, noting the Soviet military build-up and the increasingly aggressive Russian border stance, decided that further Soviet moves would have to be met head-on. Thus, it can be argued, Peking decided to "draw the line" against the Russians and ordered border patrols to increase the frequency of their movements and, when the Russians stepped out of what the Chinese defined as their proper place, to counter the Soviets with force. This argument's weakest point is the obvious disparity of total power in favor of the Russians, but along the frontier itself the balance may be have been more even and in some places in China's favor. This seems to have been the case in the vicinity of Damansky. At any rate, this argument states that the Chinese had little choice but to attempt to stop the Russians before the latter became too bold and began to occupy territory instead of merely trespassing. [pp.53–54]

Mao Zedong (on the left) and Lin Biao (on the right) at the Presidium of the 9th CPC Congress. (Chinese Internet)

'In the fight to defeat the Soviet revisionists' armed intrusion, the heroic Chinese frontier guards have fully realized [*sic*] that the Soviet revisionist renegade clique is but a paper tiger when it faces the Chinese people who, armed with Mao Tsetung [*sic*] thought, fear neither hardship nor death.' (from the pamphlet 'Down with the New Tsars!', Peking, 1969; Chinese Internet)

Robinson attempts to take the position of an impartial researcher, and, therefore, carefully makes sure that accusations against one side are immediately offset by accusations against the other side. However, this understanding of objectivity, which is so characteristic for other Western scholars as well when dealing with issues that do not concern their own countries, is completely artificial and, therefore, has nothing in common with the search for the truth. Why does he not speak about the fact that Soviet military build-up was the result of an exacerbation of the situation on the border, the blame for which lies completely with the Chinese? What aggression are we talking about – perhaps he has in mind the opposition to the Maoists' increasingly more brazen infringement into Soviet territory? Mention of Soviet occupation of certain territories should be classified in the category of 'curiosities'.

> A second possible explanation is the "pre-emption" argument, which stresses the Chinese recognition of the need to do something about the increasing disparity of forces in border military districts in favor of the Soviets. Concluding that a clash was inevitable unless the Russians were thrown off balance, Peking may have decided to initiate action in an area where the Soviets were comparatively weak, hoping to convince the Soviet Union not to proceed further in its plans.
>
> A third foreign policy explanation, the "dragon's teeth" argument, presumes that Mao was in full control of politics in China and that his policy toward the Soviet Union in 1969

continued to be based upon his view of that country as the hated and feared revisionist "enemy within" the world Communist movement. In this explanation, Mao feared that despite the overall success of four years of Cultural Revolution struggle against revisionist influence in China, the possibility remained of the re-impregnation of the revisionist virus, both internally from within the Chinese body politic and externally through Soviet influence. What was needed was a vaccination against revisionism that would hold its potency well beyond Mao's own demise. If the Chinese people could be convinced, once and for all, of the threat of Soviet revisionism, they might not be tempted again by the "bourgeois revisionist line." Perhaps Mao hoped that permanent national hatred for the Russians would follow a serious military clash, properly exploited in the press, and that anti-Soviet demonstrations held throughout the country would serve to drive the point home. Hence, this argument concludes, the Damansky incident was staged to sow "dragon's teeth" between China and Russia. [pp.54–55]

We can agree completely with Robinson's last statement: the 'dragon's teeth' sown by Mao Zedong in March 1969 are still complicating relations between Russia and China.

11
FOR WHOM AND WHY WAS THIS NECESSARY?

The overwhelming majority of researchers of the events of 1969 think that the reason for the bloodshed on the border was in no way the disputes regarding whom the islands on the Amur and Ussuri Rivers belonged to. The real reason for the Sino-Soviet Border War was the internal politics of China, which at this time was just going through the peak of the so-called 'cultural revolution'. Mao had come up with this 'revolution' in order to achieve absolute power and use unlimited authority for the comprehensive reformation of China. In Mao's opinion, the old bureaucratic cadres had to be eliminated and young, energetic and completely loyal people brought to power, which would prove the correctness of his ideas. Mao clearly thirsted for revenge for all his former economic failures; he failed once again, however, and with much more serious consequences than before. The current catastrophe was convulsing the country: the economy was collapsing, science and culture were deteriorating, the atrocities of the Red Guards were occurring everywhere, and chaos and pandemonium reigned. All this could not help but elicit in Chinese society feelings of despair, hopelessness, and disappointment in the course being followed. So then, in order to stabilise the situation and rally the people around himself in the face of an external threat (even an imaginary one), Mao organised a sharp exacerbation of relations with the USSR. In this regard, the memoirs of Mao's former personal physician are indicative. The Chinese leader said the following to him verbatim: 'If the external threat disappears, then internal strife may begin in the country.'[1]

In addition to resolving the problem of consolidating Chinese society, the experienced Mao could also see other advantageous consequences of a small border conflict.

One can number internal party affairs among such advantageous consequences, because the 9th CPC Congress, scheduled for April 1969, could have sprung unplanned surprises on the Chairman of the CC CPC. What had happened on the border probably forced into silence those who thought that the disagreements with the CPSU and the USSR could be completely overcome, inasmuch as now anyone bold enough to tell the truth about relations with the Soviet Union would immediately be branded a 'traitor' and a 'Soviet agent'.

Organisation of a conflict was also necessary for PRC Minister of Defence Lin Biao and his military entourage in order to strengthen his position, inasmuch as an armed conflict objectively pushed the congress participants into making decisions that would give the PLA leadership more rights.[2]

The fighting on the border made it possible for Mao to show the whole world that no one would succeed in doing to China what was done to Czechoslovakia in August 1968. As is known, the invasion of the latter by the Warsaw Pact armies was argued as a necessity in protecting the gains of socialism. At that time the leaders of the USSR had lost faith that Dubček and his associates would be able to resolve the problems that had arisen; therefore, they took the matter into their own hands. Mao was not afraid to clash with a formidable nuclear power, and he demonstrated the readiness of the Chinese to fight to the last man.

The war against the USSR made it possible for Mao to improve relations with the West, first and foremost the US. After all, the dead Soviet and Chinese soldiers were the most convincing proof that the ideological dispute between the CPSU and CPC was not simply a temporary argument within the family of socialist states, but rather a full rupture of relations between the USSR and PRC. It was not by chance that soon after the border events American diplomacy expanded activities to regularise relations with Peking and prepare a visit by the US president to China.

In making the decision to attack the Soviet border guards, the personal qualities of the Chinese leader played a definite role. Everyone who was close to Mao remarked on his thorough knowledge of Chinese history and literature and his commitment to and love for everything Chinese. Centuries of humiliation and oppression of the people awoke in Mao a heightened feeling of affronted dignity, which was manifested in a most bizarre way. Some negative qualities of the Chinese leader – love of power, vanity and a neglectful attitude toward the fates of people – also contributed to this.

Many books have been written about Mao Zedong in various countries, whose authors attempted to understand the character and way of thinking of this man. Possibly, however, the key is contained in the words of Mao himself, who once characterised himself as Marx and Qin Shihuang in one person. What did 'the great helmsman' have in mind?

From Marx he borrowed postulates in the spirit of *The Communist Manifesto* – rejection of private property, the idea of general communisation, etc. Therefore, Mao's accusations against the Soviet leadership were not unfounded: the latter had, in fact, moved away from the most odious dogmas of Marxism and, therefore, in the opinion of the Chinese leader, had tarnished themselves with revisionism. However, the leaders of the CPSU also logically accused

Mao of dogmatism, because Mao had not moved a single step away from the ideas of early Marxism.

The ancient Chinese leader Qin Shihuang was famous for the establishment of the centralised Qin Empire. Along the way he burned books and killed scholars. Similarly, Qin Shihuang's bloody deeds delighted Mao and were the object of emulation.

As for the Soviet leadership, no one was interested in a sharp exacerbation of relations with China – in any case, no contrary documented evidence or even personal testimonials from former highly placed persons have yet been discovered. Moscow would not even theoretically allow the possibility of shooting on the border. The political organs of the USSR border troops made it clear to their men in place that, when viewing relations with China, it was necessary to use a class approach and proceed from the principle of proletarian internationalism. It has also been said that the Soviets did not agree with the political leadership of the CPC; however, the PRC was essentially a socialist state. If the Chinese comrades had committed serious political errors, then sooner or later the healthy forces of Chinese society would inevitably rise to the top. This, they said, was the logic of historical development and the determining trend.

In the Soviet Union they assumed that in the modern era socialist countries could wage war only against the hostile capitalist encirclement. That being said, they thought it obvious that socialist countries would never be the first to attack, that they would only repel imperialist aggressors. As for the possibility of wars and armed conflicts within the socialist camp, such ideas were not even expressed hypothetically because of their absurdity.

Mao's personal activities were assessed at closed congresses and party meetings. It was said that he was allowing deviations from the principles of Marxism-Leninism, but he still was a communist. One of the main reasons for Mao's incorrect policies was the Chinese leader's personal qualities, and even his age: as they said, in everyday life Mao had simply 'become foolish in his old age'.

In confidential conversations among themselves, the most progressive Soviet citizens at times expressed the opinion that 'ours are good too' and that all the squabbling was because of the personal ambitions of the Soviet and Chinese leaders. With a certain amount of humour the subject of the dispute was specified in this way: the leaders of the CPSU and CPC cannot figure out who of them has better studied the works of Marx and Lenin.

Recently some Russian scholars have discussed the fact that the Soviet generals and directors of the military-industrial complex allegedly could have had an interest in a war. It should be acknowledged that such 'novel' hypotheses are only idle speculations. Indeed, the USSR economy was quite militarised and never experienced shortages in resources. And the war in Vietnam, which at that time was reaching its apogee, was an adequate stimulus for strengthening the defence capabilities of the Soviet Union. Thus, the Soviet military-industrial generals had no reasons whatsoever to claim additional pieces of the budgetary pie.

Another matter is that the events that had taken place could have been fully used by the leadership of the CPSU and USSR as a reason for bringing a certain discipline into the socialist camp. However, this is already another issue, in no way associated with identifying those to blame for the bloodshed on the border.

American scholar Thomas Robinson, who has already been cited in the previous chapter, also found no proof that anyone from the Soviet leadership was interested in a war against China. Nevertheless, he tries to find at least some signs of such interest or even individual phrases from officials and writers that indicate the existence of such signs. For this, Robinson attentively looked into Soviet publications – so intently that at times he saw something that the authors themselves did not see. The American focused particular attention on articles in the journal *Armed Forces Communist* [*Kommunist Vooruzhennykh Sil/KVS*]:

> First, there was an attempt to tar Maoist China with the imperialist brush, so that arguments against imperialism, the main external enemy of the socialist '"commonwealth", might also be used against China. Second, and more important, there was an attempt to extend the Brezhnev doctrine to deal with "leftism", the main enemy inside the camp. The Brezhnev doctrine can be stated positively, neutrally, or negatively, depending on the degree of threat to the "gains of socialism" one sees in a given country. When the situation becomes so serious that a "direct threat" to the gains of socialism exists, action must be taken to prevent further deterioration and to restore the *status quo ante*. Although the doctrine usually referred to the Czechoslovak case, several of the *KVS* articles either mentioned China in the same context or implied that the doctrine in its negative sense must be applied to China. Since Maoist policy has brought a threat to socialist gains in China, it may be necessary to "extirpate" such "leftist" deviationists. This is particularly true when the "imperialist" enemy without, which poses an increasing, direct threat to socialism, allies itself with the deviationist enemy within. One must then move to eliminate the latter in order to block the attack from the former.[3]

Thus, Robinson presents a possible way of thinking with regard to the Soviet leaders. In his opinion, a theoretical foundation of a military operation against the Chinese had already been developed:

> Thus these several military writers set the theoretical stage for military action against China. Since their articles antedated the first March incident, it is possible that some sectors of the Soviet armed forces, in alliance with some Party officials, were pushing for a showdown with China. It is of course impossible to say whether this affected the events leading to the first violent outbreak.[4]

Nevertheless, Robinson rejects the theory that the Soviet leadership had any foreign policy reasons for exacerbating relations with China:

> From the Soviet invasion of Czechoslovakia in August 1968 through February 1969, the Russians were preoccupied with Eastern European problems. The Arab-Israeli conflict also occupied Moscow's attention, as the Kremlin attempted to prevent its client states from entering another unwinnable war, which would also threaten the Soviet Union with direct confrontation with the United States. Strategic issues, too – strategic arms limitations talks and the question of escalation of the arms race through competitive antiballistic missile systems – were matters of concern. The September and November Budapest meetings of the Preparatory Committee for the long-postponed International Communist Conference claimed some attention. Treatment of Communists in Indonesia, NATO and sea power in the Mediterranean, and Yugoslav revisionism claimed attention in Moscow.[5]

Chen Xilian. (Chinese Internet)

Xiao Quanfu. (Chinese Internet)

Finally, Robinson's general conclusion was presented as follows: 'The possibility that the Russians, not the Chinese, took preemptive [*sic*] action and initiated the 2 March incident is so remote that we reject it.'[6]

It is interesting: what was the opinion of the Chinese themselves – not of the leaders or the full-time propagandists, but of some of those servicemen who knew about the 2 March 1969 events?

A former PLA commando, previously cited, writes the following:

> What was the actual reason for this border war? Who began it? Both sides accuse each other; however, for a correct understanding of the 1969 Sino-Soviet border dispute it is first necessary to understand the social and political situation at that time.
>
> It is well known that, after a long struggle, the Communist Party of China first gained power in 1949. It is much less known that the Soviet Union played a key role in this. In 1945 Soviet troops attacked the Japanese and liberated Manchuria at lightning speed. Monuments to the Soviet liberating forces can still be seen in these places. The USSR then made it possible for the PLA to enter Manchuria and armed it with captured Japanese weapons, and also trained the troops. This directly accelerated the liberation of China. However, in 1960 relations began to worsen, because Chairman Mao began to fear the Soviet Union's enormous influence. In order to distract the people's attention from domestic problems caused by the Cultural Revolution (1966-1969), Mao Zedong announced that the Soviet Union was the immediate threat to the nation. This immediately moved the PLA into a war against the Soviet border units along the northern border.[7]

Contemporary China is not silent about the fact itself of the war; that being said, however, once again they are trying not to remember it. Official treatment of what took place for the most part repeats the propaganda clichés of the time of the 'cultural revolution'. For example, the Chinese, without exception, are listed in the ranks of heroes, while, as mentioned before, the treacherous 2 March 1969 attack against the Soviet border guards is called 'a self-defence counterattack'.

At the same time, some Chinese researchers have concluded that it was the Chinese who provoked the armed clash, and, what is more, that it was carefully planned. Chinese historian Yang Kuisong says that in 1968 the Central Military Commission, headed by Mao, was already discussing the situation on the border with the USSR. As a result of these discussions, instructions were prepared for the commands of the Shenyang and Peking Military Districts. The main thing in these instructions was an order to prepare a military operation against the USSR as a means of strengthening China's diplomatic position in talks with the Soviet leadership.[8]

In carrying out Peking's order, the Shenyang Military District command prepared a small detachment of selected servicemen, assigned to attack the Soviet border guards. This detachment was covertly moved to the region of Kirkinsky Island (three kilometres north of Damansky), with the task of mounting a surprise attack against the Soviet troops in case of another border incident. At that time, however, an appropriate instance had not presented itself.

Subsequently, the attack plan was adjusted a few times; not only PLA General Staff officers, but also staff from the MFA were enlisted for this matter.

Finally, the Chinese specified a new place for the attack – Damansky Island. A group of commanders, headed by Chief of Staff of the Military Subdistrict Wang Ziliang, was deployed to the Hunzy border post; Xiao Quanfu was designated as responsible for the operation.

General Chen Xilian, former commander of the Shenyang Military District, attests to the reliability of everything that was said above. He writes:

> For two to three months, we had been preparing for the first battle (the battle of 2 March). From among the units of three armies, we selected three reconnaissance companies, each of which was composed of two to three hundred soldiers and commanded by army staff members with combat experience. We provided them with special equipment and special training, and then dispatched them secretly to take position on the [Zhenbao] island in advance. When the Soviet troops attempted their provocation on 2 March, they actually were hopelessly outnumbered by us. We won a clear victory on the battlefield.[9]

The Chinese journal *World Knowledge* (2006, No. 13) published a very illustrative article '1966-1976: Isolation Is Replaced by Openness'. In the article several historians discuss events from the time of the 'cultural revolution'. In particular Professor Li Danhui saw the main reason for the escalation on the border being the treaty that the USSR concluded with Mongolia. Nevertheless, she had to have known well that the Chinese provocations on the Soviet border had already begun in 1960, which forced the Soviets to take measures to strengthen their eastern borders. However, attempts to whitewash 'her own' do not merit special attention. It is more important that Li Danhui gave a completely definitive answer to the question as to who organised the bloodshed on the border. The article said the following:

> Simultaneously with this, tension on the Sino-Soviet border increased. In the situation of the radical left "cultural revolution" in an atmosphere of a bitter anti-revisionist struggle, which had penetrated Chinese society from top to bottom, the following plan for military measures on the border was quickly adopted: after selecting an appropriate time and place, to attack the Soviet troops who were obstructing the arrival of Chinese border troops on the islands; to not worry that the clash would escalate into a serious conflict and full-scale war. At the same time, the CPC was getting ready for the IX Congress. Mao Zedong assumed that the attack against the Soviet troops on the eve of the congress would contribute to the development of the policy of struggle against revisionism, make it possible to rally the party, and put an end to factionalism; he was stabilising the situation in the country. During the first Sino-Soviet talks on the border issue, however, it was planned to turn Zhenbaodao over to China. The Soviet Union would not have made an aggravated negative response to actions regarding this island. On the other hand, Soviet border troops had controlled the island since 1947, i.e., for more than 20 years. Organising an attack in just this place might produce a much greater effect than in other islands. On the whole, the measure was to cause a tumultuous response and contribute to the further exacerbation of the situation; however, that being said, it was also necessary to worry about their own security. The plan of attack on Zhenbaodao was developed, based on these considerations. Beginning at the end of February 1969, with the approval of Mao Zedong and the CC CPC, China systematically and covertly prepared a counterattack in the region of the island. In March, war broke out on Zhenbaodao.[10]

Thus, for three decades Chinese propaganda hid the truth about those responsible for the Damansky tragedy, and now – as they say, without any smooth transition – some historians are allowed to say what actually happened on 2 March 1969. That being said, however, the official treatment of the events remains as before, with reference to publications that very few people – mainly researchers and those interested in the subject of the Sino-Soviet war – know. As for ordinary citizens, they, as before, are presented with the lies of the 'cultural revolution' days. The following illustrates this.

Recently, Chinese media have noted the growth of the influence and popularity of the internet company Sohu. A certain Mao Xinren, one of the authors who are often published on this company's site and who runs a blog with 120 million followers, decided to open the eyes of his readers on the events of 50 years ago. The title of the article – 'Truth and Fiction about the Border Conflict on Damansky Island: the USSR and China Had to Pay Dearly' – greatly obligated the author.[11] One can tell that Mao Xinren had deeply delved into the topic, separated the truth from fiction, and now hurried to share his discoveries with his readers.

Alas, when reading the first paragraph the impression arises that the author has only superficially looked at publications in the tabloid press, and then thoughtlessly listed any ravings in these publications, such as the fact that the border events were the result of a conspiracy between PRC Minister of Defence Lin Biao and unnamed Soviet politicians. Further on, he himself expresses his doubts about this, etc. Finally, he comes to well-known statements of the type 'the USSR did not want to listen to warnings and protests, and the provocations continued'; 'the Chinese were forced to counterattack for the purpose of self-defence', and so on – in general, word for word as in 1969. That being said, some of his statements are laughable. For example, mentioning the battle of 15 March 1969 (which we will discuss in Volume 2), he writes: 'In repelling the attack, the division commander, Colonel Leonov, and Lieutenant Colonel Yanshin were killed.' If Mao Xinren is purely a civilian, then his lack of understanding of the difference between a division commander and chief of a border detachment is completely forgivable. But only a person who has not studied anything, but has simply taken the first piece of propaganda from the 'cultural revolution' that has fallen into his hands, and has published this as his article, can say that Lieutenant Colonel Yanshin died in the battle on Damansky. After all, it would have been enough for Mao Xinren just to have taken a look at the internet to find out that after the fighting on the border Ye.I. Yanshin was awarded the Order of Lenin, served for a long time on the western border of the USSR, and died in Brest (today, part of the Republic of Belarus) in 2009 at the age of 79.

It seems that today's Chinese leaders are favourably inclined toward the 'oeuvre' of such authors, who are ready to parrot any nonsense, if only to be afloat in the media. The capabilities of the internet make it possible for interested Chinese citizens to find out many new things about the 1969 events, and the Chinese authorities can no longer be an obstacle to this.

12 MOSCOW – PEKING

For a long time the political leadership of the USSR hid the disagreements with China from the country's ordinary communists and citizens. At the beginning of the 1960s they began to talk about this aloud; however, even now the Kremlin has been attempting as much as possible to limit the scope of the polemics. It was thought that the disagreements were temporary, and often subjective, and, therefore, there was no reason to exacerbate relations, which would have delighted world imperialism.

In 1964 a 'change of watch' occurred in the Soviet Union: L.I. Brezhnev replaced the ousted N.S. Khrushchev. Yesterday's party comrades and friends accused the disgraced Nikita Sergeyevich of all mortal sins, one of which was the damaged relations with China.

Protests in the USSR, March 1969. (photo© The Khabarovsk Territorial Museum after N.I. Grodekov)

Some former colleagues from the CC CPSU were now saying that the new Soviet leadership was undertaking efforts to normalise relations with Peking, but the inertia of the past was telling, and, therefore, nothing had come of this. It could have been that way, to some degree, but old disputes could hardly have been the main reason for the further exacerbation of relations. After all, in the 1960s Mao had plunged his country into a series of misfortunes, in the context of which relations with the USSR by no means looked like a matter of prime importance. Thus, the direct confrontation with the USSR was not a consequence of old grievances, but rather part of a deliberate game on the part of Chairman Mao. As for the changes in the personnel make-up of the Soviet leadership, these were not so important: practically all of those who went along with Khrushchev in the squabbling with China still remained in their posts.

It would be naïve to think that the Brezhnev leadership was exclusively engaged in deals. Seeing that relations with China were getting worse, Moscow took measures. Foreign researchers have written about some of them. For example, S. F. Ostermann writes the following:

> The new Soviet leadership, headed by Leonid Brezhnev (who overthrew Khrushchev in October 1964), reacted to Peking's confrontational pose by intensifying economic and military pressure. At the early stage of confrontation, the Soviets recalled vitally important personnel and advisors from the PRC. Moscow also initiated a long-term build-up of the armed forces in the Soviet Far East. Soviet forces sharply increased after 1965 – from 17 divisions to 27 divisions by 1969 (and as many as 48 divisions by the mid-1970s). Moscow also decided to deploy the SS-4 mid-range ballistic missiles (SCUD and FROG). Other initiatives had the aim of strengthening border control along the border with the PRC. Having increased geostrategic pressure on Peking, Moscow also concluded a 20-year friendship treaty with Mongolia. The treaty envisioned joint Soviet-Mongolian defence efforts and the deployment of two or three Soviet divisions in the People's Republic of Mongolia.[1]

All the same, the 2 March 1969 events resounded in Moscow like thunder in a clear sky. The Kremlin was now forced to thrust aside all standards of communist etiquette and explain to the Soviet people how and why our closest neighbour and friend had gone to war against us. At the same time, it was necessary to rally the people so that no citizens would doubt the correctness of the CPSU's policies.

The 2 March 1969 notes from the Soviet government to the PRC government were carefully read in local party committees. Experienced *apparatchiks* knew: it was clearly and precisely indicated there, where attention was to be focused in the unfolding campaign.

After a brief summary, without details, of what had taken place, the note included the following statements:

> 1. The organisers of the provocation were the Chinese authorities, and the purpose of the provocation was to exacerbate the situation.
> 2. Henceforth, provocateurs will be repelled, and the responsibility for all possible consequences lay on the Chinese government.
> 3. The Chinese people are in no way to blame.

The note reported that there were dead and wounded on the Soviet side; however, specific numbers were not cited. For the most perceptive readers, this served as a signal that the casualties were significant. Generally, the note said nothing about dead Chinese, and this gave rise to an incorrect perception of what had happened: that the Chinese had attacked, killed an unknown number of Soviet soldiers and then simply gone on their way. Many ordinary Soviet citizens were surprised: was this because of the helplessness of our soldiers?! For several days there was no new information about what had happened on Damansky; there was only a brief report about the burial of the victims of the fighting, which had taken place on 6 March.

Unexpectedly, on 7 March the USSR MFA organised a press conference at which Chief of the Press Department L.M. Zamyatin for the first time officially announced the number of Soviet casualties: 31 border troops dead and 14 wounded. Later, Zamyatin and General Lieutenant P.I. Ionov, deputy chief of the USSR Main Border Troops Directorate, answered many of the correspondents' questions.

On the same day a protest was held at the Chinese embassy in Moscow. Well-organised convoys of workers, students, engineer and technical workers, representatives of the *intelligentsia* and other categories of citizens arrived at the Chinese embassy to protest against those responsible for the bloodshed. The protesters carried banners on which slogans had been written, the most typical of them being: 'Down with the Mao Zedong clique!' 'The Soviet borders are impenetrable!' 'Shame on the Peking provocateurs!' 'Mao's policies are a tragedy for China!', 'The Soviet people are always with the CPSU!' etc. From time to time the people chanted slogans and simultaneously raised their clenched fists above their heads.

Some of the protest's participants recall that 7 March 1969 was hardly the only day in Soviet history when the police permitted hooliganism. Young people, mainly students, came to the embassy gate with vials of ink and used them to visibly damage the diplomatic mission's building. Each successful hit was accompanied by shouts of approval and applause. It was as if the embassy had been deserted: windows were tightly curtained, no one came out into the yard...

According to estimates, 50,000 people took part in the protest at the PRC embassy.

The protest at the Chinese embassy continued on 8 March. The number of demonstrators was considerably larger – as many as 100,000 people. This time the people were really angry: everyone knew the number of dead and the circumstances of the provocation. The crowd that had gathered chanted as a chorus 'Shame! Shame! Shame!' and stuck poles with banners in the snow near the embassy gate. TASS described the episode as follows:

> The risky policies of the Mao Zedong clique, the consequence of which was the armed provocation on the Sino-Soviet border, are being confronted by the decisive judgement of all Soviet people.
>
> On 8 March, as on the day before, thousands of blue- and white-collar workers, and representatives of the *intelligentsia* gathered near the Chinese embassy building in Moscow to angrily protest the provocative actions of the Peking authorities on the Sino-Soviet border. Outrage is on their faces. Many are carrying banners: 'Provocateurs – to the pillory!' 'We completely approve of the measures by the Soviet government!', 'Down with the chauvinistic policies of the Mao Zedong clique!', 'Long live the CPSU and its Leninist Central Committee!'
>
> The fists of the demonstrators are angrily raised, and moral outrage aimed at the representatives of Mao Zedong's bankrupt leadership can be heard.[2]

The Soviet press and television focused specific attention on the events on the border, but it cannot be said that materials about

Protests in China, March 1969. (from the pamphlet 'Down with the New Tsars!', Peking, 1969; Chinese Internet)

Damansky were printed exclusively on the front pages of newspapers and journals. A characteristic detail is that not a single newspaper published a map of the area in the region of Damansky Island, because then it would have been clear how close the island was to the Chinese riverbank. Instead, a little later it was muttered that in the Damansky region the border ran along the Chinese riverbank. It is true that Soviet television showed a panorama of the island, taken from a helicopter, but even in this case the perspective made it impossible to gauge the actual distances in the area (by the way, Chinese newspapers published maps of the area).

A wave of protests and meetings swept throughout the entire country, at which the Soviet people were sincerely outraged about the actions of the Chinese authorities who organised the armed provocation on the border. The party leadership gave the tone and direction of the measures being taken.

Ordinary citizens completely agreed with such assessments; however, they grieved much more about the victims than about the actual rift with China. Awareness that such young Soviet lads died in peacetime and on their own soil elicited real hatred towards the organisers of the Damansky exploit. The following are some typical examples.[3]

A meeting was held at the Lenin Komsomol Automobile Factory (Moscow). Assembly line worker V. Svistunova spoke:

> I am deeply outraged at the vile tricks of the Chinese provocateurs. The monstrous crime has brought forth pain and protest of all Soviet people. Young lads and Komsomol members, who should still be living and loving, were killed and wounded . . . This is slanderous villainy, of which the evilest enemies of humanity are capable. Among them is the Mao Zedong clique. But they forgot the old adage: 'Whoever comes against us with a sword will perish by the sword.'

Around 300 people gathered in workshop number 7 of the Novogroznensky Petroleum Refinery. Secretary of the Komsomol Committee V. Savinkov spoke:

> The minions of Mao Zedong turned to military provocations. This was playing with fire. The Soviet people are patient for the time being. The Komsomol members and young people of our refinery are expressing their deep outrage at the malicious venture by the Peking authorities... If necessary, we will stand with weapons in our hands for the protection of our Motherland and the gains of Great October.

Servicemen of the Taman Division wrote an open letter to the Far East border guards:

> We are amazed by your courage and your bravery, which you demonstrated in repelling the armed bandit raid that was organised by the Chinese authorities. This raid cost the lives of 31 border guard warriors and 14 men were wounded. You fought, without sparing your lives, protecting the state border of the Soviet Union and with decisive actions you stopped the naked provocation. We are proud of you and with you mourn our brothers-in-arms. The blood of Soviet soldiers that flows on the banks of the Ussuri will not be forgotten.

The party leadership of the USSR followed the course of the campaign and was sensitive to the slightest nuances. The people began to talk about how 'little the damned Chinese got in return', and that 'we should make it so there is no trace left'. A directive response followed immediately (in the spirit of the 2 March note):

> The actions of Mao Zedong and his cohorts, which threaten the socialist gains of the workers of China, are directed not only against the Soviet people, but also against the Chinese people (from an announcement by the Central Governing Board of the Sino-Soviet Friendship Society).
>
> The Soviet people do not identify the frenzied Maoists with the Chinese people (from a talk by senior lecturer A. Budyan at a rally at the Kishinev Polytechnical Institute).
>
> We know the Chinese as a great and hard-working people, who have created a wonderful culture and literature. And we are insulted when, under the guise of 'cultural revolution', the spirit of the people is trampled. We have never equated the workers China with the Mao Zedong clique (from a letter by academician P. Glebka).'

A propaganda campaign also unfolded in China, one that was quite similar to the Soviet one. Practically the same methods were used – naturally with an 180 degree turn in the search for those responsible for the bloodshed: people gathered at protests and demonstrations at the Soviet embassy in Peking, citizens wrote letters to newspapers and to higher authorities, etc. The slogans most often used were 'Dirty provocation of the enemies of China!', 'Down with American imperialism and Soviet revisionism!' and 'Down with the new tsars!'

What was somewhat different in the Chinese variant was the extreme hysteria of the participants, the much cruder work of the propaganda apparatus, the sheer poverty of the discourse or the complete lack of it. The latter was mostly explained by the lesser experience of the Chinese political commentators and the substantially lower educational level of the Chinese people. For example, on 4 March 1969 an editorial appeared in the PRC's main newspaper, *The People's Daily*, and the PLA newspaper, *The People's Liberation Army Daily*, which laid out the PRC leadership's attitude toward what had happened on the border. The following are some excerpts from this editorial:

> On 2 March, the Soviet revisionist renegade clique sent armed soldiers to flagrantly intrude into Chenpao Island on the Wusili River, Heilungkiang Province, China, and killed and wounded many frontier guards of the Chinese People's Liberation Army by opening up with cannon and gun fire on them. This is an extremely grave armed border provocation carried out by the Soviet revisionists, a frantic anti-China incident created by them and another big exposure of the rapacious nature of Soviet revisionism as social imperialism. The Chinese people and the Chinese People's Liberation Army express the greatest indignation at this towering crime committed by the Soviet revisionist renegade clique and voice the strongest protest against it...
>
> The Soviet revisionist renegade clique's armed provocation against our country is a frenzied action that has been taken out of the need of its domestic and foreign policies at a time when it is beset with difficulties at home and abroad and has landed in an impasse. In doing so, it tries to whip up anti-China sentiments for the purpose of diverting the attention of the Soviet people whose resentment and resistance against its reactionary bourgeois fascist rule are growing daily and, at the same time, to please US imperialism and curry favour with the newly installed Nixon administration so that the United States and the Soviet Union may

> enter into further counter-revolutionary deals on a global scale. The Soviet revisionist renegade clique thought that it would get out of its predicament by creating a new anti-China incident. But the result is just the opposite. There is a profound revolutionary friendship between the peoples of China and the Soviet Union and all the anti-China schemes of the Soviet revisionist renegade clique are bound to go bankrupt completely. This perverse action of the Soviet revisionist renegade clique only serves to reveal its counter-revolutionary features still more clearly and arouse even stronger opposition from the Soviet people and the people all over the world. In lifting a rock only to drop it on its own feet, the Soviet revisionist renegade clique will only hasten its own destruction.[4]

In reading these pieces, one cannot immediately grasp who, in the opinion of Peking, are the leaders of the USSR: traitors, renegades, revisionists, or the former two or all three simultaneously. Strictly speaking, at that time this was not important: the main thing was that all the Chinese people, as chorus, repeated this *abracadabra* and thought less about the substantive side of the matter.

The events on the Ussuri caused extensive responses in other countries. Western mass media attempted to make as fair an assessment as possible of what had happened; however, they were faced with a clear shortage of accurate information. For this reason they only quoted announcements by both sides of the conflict and attempted to forecast the future development of events. Naturally, they did not miss the opportunity to once again bad-mouth the behaviour and habits in communist countries.

The leaders and press of the majority of socialist states unambiguously took the side of the USSR: the assessments they gave were completely the same as the Soviet assessments. In particular, informing the leaders of socialist countries in a timely fashion about what was happening on the border contributed to this.

A curious document was found in the archives of the former GDR; it had been sent from Moscow to the East German leaders on 8 March 1969.[5] There were a total of five copies of this dispatch, and one can assume with great probability that four of them were designated for Walter Ulbricht, Willi Stoph, Erich Honecker and Herman Achen. Most likely P.A. Abrasimov, USSR ambassador to the GDR, received the fifth copy.

The dispatch contained both a summary of the border events and an assessment made by the Soviet leadership regarding relations with China.[6] In compiling the text of the dispatch, diplomatic documents and materials from the Moscow press conferences that had been convened for Soviet and foreign journalists were used. Several phrases in all these papers coincided word for word. In addition, the dispatch also contained some new information – in particular, an assessment was made of the economic importance of Damansky, information was provided about its geographic position, etc. A considerable portion of the document was set aside for the role of the Chinese leadership in the world communist movement.

In the context of the common opinion of the majority of the socialist countries, Albania, Yugoslavia, and Romania occupy a special position. North Korea's position also merits special mention.

At the beginning of the 1960s, Albanian leader Enver Hoxha had already taken a course of self-isolation for his country and, at the same time, close ties with China. He apparently hoped to raise the country's economy with the help of China, which would have been given in thanks for Tirana's anti-Soviet position. China did, in fact, help Albania, but on a scale that was far from what Hoxha had hoped for. True or not, the following words are ascribed to Hoxha, with which he supposedly reproached the Chinese: 'To build communism in Albania, it would be enough if each Chinese person did not eat breakfast one time.'

The first friction between the Albanian and Chinese leaders arose at the end of the 1960s and after US President Nixon's visit to the PRC, Hoxha directly declared to Mao that the logic of 'the enemy of my enemy is my friend' could not be applied in this case. Hoxha considered the Soviet leadership to be revisionist, but all the same viewed the USSR as a socialist state. In his opinion, the US was and remained a hostile imperialist power. The disagreements that had arisen finally led to a complete rift in relations between Albania and China in 1978.

It is entirely possible that Mao expected moral support from Josip Broz Tito, and he had good reasons for this. The fact is that six months before the events on the Ussuri, Tito had openly criticised the Soviet leadership for the invasion of Czechoslovakia. Counter-accusations were heard in response: it was said that Tito supported counterrevolution, and that Yugoslavia's political and economic system had little in common with socialism. That being said, however, the sides refrained from vulgarity and offensive characterisations.

In the case of Damansky, Tito did not think it expedient to take one of the sides in the conflict too explicitly, inasmuch as for a long time he had seen himself as the leader of the nonalignment movement. He also remembered that the Chinese had renounced him as an ally in 1948, after the split with Stalin. And in the USSR they well remembered another thing: how much effort had been required to smooth relations with Yugoslavia after several years of hostility. Therefore, they refrained from criticism that might go beyond the bounds of decency.

The situation with Romania was somewhat different, inasmuch as this country was a member of the Warsaw Pact and had the right to vote there. Nikolai Ceausescu tried as much as possible to hold his own opinion and bring it to the attention of his comrades from 'fraternal parties'. This often irritated Moscow as, for example, regarding the 1968 events in Czechoslovakia. The armed confrontation on Damansky and its assessment did not contribute to the mutual understanding between the leaders of the CPSU and the Communist Party of Romania. Ceausescu's position was that the conflict on the Ussuri and the public polemics between the USSR and the PRC were harmful to the business of socialism, and, therefore, it was necessary to put an end to this as soon as possible. It seems that it was just at this time that there appeared a semi-official definition of Romanian politics, which Soviet propagandists used: 'The Romanians think one thing, say another, and do a third'. However it was, the Soviet leadership tried to pay less attention to Ceausescu's free-thinking, viewing it as a whim that, while not harmless, was still tolerable. Relations between Moscow and Bucharest at that time could most accurately be characterised as cool.

North Korean leader Kim Il Sung and the regime he created could exist only thanks to the USSR and China. It was these two countries that saved Kim after he attacked South Korea, but then suffered defeat after defeat after the Americans intervened. The USSR assisted with weapons and pilots, and China moved a whole army into Korea, under the command of the renowned Marshal Peng Dehuai. Hundreds of thousands of so-called 'Chinese People's Volunteers' died in the fighting, including Mao's son – this was the price that had to be paid to maintain Kim Il Sung's regime.

After the end of the war the USSR and China provided substantial economic aid to North Korea, supporting the rapid development of

North Korean industry. The reverse side of this aid was Soviet and Chinese influence, with which Kim was burdened.

The acute conflict between his 'sponsors' gave Kim the opportunity to free himself from too tight control, but, that being said, it forced the Korean leader to act extremely subtly. It is understandable that Kim wanted to maintain a position in which goods, raw materials, weapons and money continued to arrive from China and the USSR. Kim saw Moscow's and Peking's acknowledgement of him as an equal partner as a new element in their relations. Kim must be given his due: he solved both problems.

At the end of the 1950s and beginning of the 1960s, the North Korean leadership slanted in the Chinese direction. Not only the ethnic and cultural closeness of the Korean and Chinese people, but also the same (that is, negative) attitude toward the new trends from Moscow contributed to this. This especially concerned the criticism of Stalin, which had emerged in the USSR, and the new thesis about the necessity of peaceful coexistence with the capitalist countries. It was at this time that Kim expressed almost complete solidarity with Mao's foreign policy, while in the Korean press there appeared articles denouncing Moscow.

The Soviet leadership had no patience with such an attitude. The Kremlin assumed that the Soviet Union had done so much for Kim that he should be thanking his northern neighbour for as long as he lived. And if the Korean leader began to misbehave, he had to be put in his place. As a measure of pressure, it was decided to sharply reduce military and economic aid, which was immediately felt in North Korea.

At the same time, the 'cultural revolution' had emerged in China, which forced Kim to seriously think. Of course, the absurd deification of Chairman Mao and all the nonsense in China's national economy did not worry him much. However, his neighbour's chaos put Kim on his guard, inasmuch as he always was striving for order and discipline. Moreover, the unbridled Red Guards began to vilify the Korean regime and its leader in all possible ways, which literally infuriated 'the father of the Korean nation'.

Publications in the North Korean press were a clear sign of changes in Kim's position. At first there was unsigned criticism of 'dogmatism' and 'opportunism', and then articles appeared that directly condemned the policies of 'the great proletarian cultural revolution'. The Soviet leadership correctly understood the situation and quickly re-established its former relations with North Korea. No trace remained of a slant toward China in Pyongyang's policies.

Subsequently, leaders of the USSR and China attempted to persuade Kim to more clearly select between the Soviet Union and the PRC; however, he skilfully manoeuvred and occupied a neutral position. As a result, North Korea continued to obtain aid from both countries, without tying itself to any specific obligations.

It is difficult to say what Kim's attitude actually was toward the news about the war on the Ussuri. Even now it is difficult to determine if the North Korean press reported about these events in general. What is clear is that Kim not only did not want to quarrel with either side, but also wanted to protect his people from what in his opinion was unnecessary information about the surrounding world.

During those March days of 1969, no one – neither the leaders of the communist powers nor the ordinary citizens – knew yet that the events of 2 March were a prelude to a larger battle. It would break out in the middle of the month, and the victims would be numbered in the hundreds.

BIBLIOGRAPHY

Books

Anon., *Collection of Treaties between Russia and Other States. 1856-1917* (Сборник договоров России с другими государствами. 1856-1917 [in Russian]) (Moscow: Publisher unknown, 1952)

Anon., *Learn from the Battle Heroes of Zhenbao Island* (Учитесь у боевых героев Острова Чжэеньбао, [in Russian, translated from Chinese]) (Xinhua Bookstore of Liaoning Province, Liaoning People's Art Printing Factory, 1970)

Anon., *Russia's Border Troops in Wars and Military Conflicts of the 20th Century* (Пограничные войска в войнах и вооруженных конфликтах XX века [in Russian]) (Moscow: Granitsa, 2000)

Belyavskaya, V.F. (author-compiler), *Border Guards* (Пограничники [in Russian]) (Minsk: Publisher unknown, 1998)

Brezhnev, A.A., *China: The Thorny Path to Good Neighbourliness* (Китай: тернистый путь к добрососедству [in Russian]) (Moscow: Mezhdunarodnye otnosheniya, 1998)

Bubenin, V.D., *The Bloody Snow of Damansky* (Кровавый снег Даманского [in Russian]) (Moscow: Kuchkove pole, 2004)

Defense Intelligence Agency, *Handbook of the Chinese People's Liberation Army*, DDB-2680-32-84, 1984

Drozdov, Yu.I., *Notes from a Chief of Illegal Intelligence* (Записки начальника нелегальной разведки [in Russian]) (Moscow: Olma-Press, 2000)

Galenovich, Yu.M., *Russia and China in the 20th Century. The Border* (Россия и Китай в XX веке. Граница [in Russian]) (Moscow: Izograf, 2001)

Galenovich, Yu.M., *Russia—China: Six Treaties* (Россия–Китай: шесть договоров [in Russian]) (Moscow: Muravey, 2003)

Gladkov, V. and Musalov, A., *The Uneasy Border. 1969* (Неспокойная граница. Год 1969-й [in Russian]) (Moscow: Granitsa, 2018)

Kapitsa, M.S., *At Different Parallels. Notes of a Diplomat* (На разных параллелях. Записки дипломата [in Russian]) (Moscow: AO "Kniga i biznes," 1996)

Kholmogorov, M. (compiler), *Heroes of Damansky Island* (Герои острова Даманский [in Russian]) (Moscow: Molodaya gvaardiya, 1969)

Leonova, Ye.D and Murin, V.B., *Demokrat Leonov: a Life in the Name of Duty* (Демократ Леонов: жизнь во имя долга [in Russian]) (Moscow: Granitsa, 2016)

Lukashin, V., *The Heroes of Damansky* (Герои Даманского [in Russian]) (Moscow: Izvestiya, 1969)

Ministry of Defense of the USSR, *Soviet Military Encyclopaedia* (Советская военная энциклопедия [in Russian]), Vol. 3 (Moscow: Voyenizdat, 1979)

Musalov, A., *Damansky and Zhalanashkol. The 1969 Sino-Soviet Armed Conflict* (Даманский и Жаланашколь. Советско-китайский вооруженный конфликт 1969 года [in Russian]) (Moscow: Izdatelskii tsentr 'Eksprint,' 2005)

Petrov, I.I., *The Sino-Soviet Wars. The Truth about Damansky* (Советско-китайские войны. Правда о Даманском [in Russian]) (Moscow: 'Eksmo': 'Yauza,' 2009)

Razmazin, P., *Damansky. Our Pain. Sorrow. Memory . . .* (Даманский. Наше боль. Скорбь. Память . . . [in Russian]), a project of P. Razmazin (Dalnerechensk: B.M.I., 1999)

Robinson, Thomas, 'The People's Republic. Part 2. Revolutions within the Chinese Revolution, 1966-1982,' in various authors, *The Cambridge History of China* (Cambridge University Press: Cambridge, 1992) Vol. 15

Robinson, T. W., *The Sino-Soviet Border Dispute: Background, Development, and the March 1969 Clashes*, Rand Corporation Research Memorandum RM-6171-PR, 1970.

Ryabushkin, D.S., *Damansky Island. The Border Conflict. March 1969* (Остров Даманский. Пограничный конфликт. Март 1969 года [in Russian]) (Moscow: Fond 'Russkiye Vityazi,' 2015)

Ryabushkin, D.S., *It Was on Damansky* (Это было на Даманском [in Russian]) (Kazan: Publisher unknown, 2019)

Ryabushkin, D.S., *Myths of Damansky* (Мифы Даманского [in Russian]) (Moscow: AST, 2004)

Ryabushkin, D.S., 'Origins and Consequences of the Soviet–Chinese Border Conflict of 1969,' in Akihiro, Iwashita, *Eager Eyes Fixed on Eurasia* (Sapporo: Slavic Research Center, Hokkaido University, 2007), pp.73–91

Sabadash, A.A. et al., *Transcripts of Conversations with Veterans of the War on Damansky Island V.I. Abramov, A.S. Belozerov, M.T. Vashchenko, G.A. Kuzminykh, N.I. Nikiferov, V.S. Prosvirnikov, N.I. Ruban, V.P. Fateyev, A.I. Filimonov, 2002-2003* (Стенограммы бесед с участниками конфликта на острове Даманском В.И. Абрамовым, А.С. Белсеровым, М.Т. Ващенко, Г.А. Кузминых, Н.И. Никеферовым, В.С. Просвирниковым, Н.И. Рубаном, В.П. Фатеевым, А. И. Филимоновым, 2003-2004 [in Russian]) (unpublished)

Streltsov, D.V. (ed.), *The Territorial Issue in the Afro-Asian World* (Территориальный вопрос в афро-азиатском мире [in Russian]) (Moscow: Aspent Press, 2013)

Sviderskiy, N.G., 'Facets of Character' (Грани характера [in Russian]), in Anon., *Heroes of the Far eastern Borders (Collection of Materials on the Defenders of Damansky Island)* (Герои рубежей дальневосточных (Сборник материалов о защитниках острова Даманский) [in Russian]) (Khabarovsk: Publisher unknown, 1969)

Vashchenko, M.T. and Knyazev, A.L., (compilers), *Island of Bravery. Recollections of Veterans of the Combat Operations on Damansky Island* (Остров мужества. Воспоминания участников боевых действий на о. Даманский [in Russian]) (Khabarovsk: izdatel'stvo 'RIOTIP' kraevoy tipografii, 2006)

Yakovets, A.P., (compiler), *Damansky. This Is How It Was. The 50th Anniversary of the Border Conflict on the Ussuri River. 1969-2019* (Даманский. Так это было. 50 лет пограничному конфликту на реке Уссури. 1969-2019 [in Russian]), 2nd edition, corrected and supplemented: album (Vladivostok: Russkii ostrov, 2019)

Zhibin, Chen and Xiaozhu, Sun, *Confrontation at the Freezing Point: Record of the 1962-1969 Sino-Soviet Border Battles* (Конфронтация при замораживании: запись советско-китайской пограничной битвы с 1962 по 1969 год [in Russian, translated from Chinese]) (Beijing: International Cultural Publication Company, 1992)

Zhisui, Li, *Notes of a Personal Physician* (Записки личного врача [in Russian]), Book 1 (Minsk: Inter-Digest, Smolensk: TOO Ekho, 1996)

Periodical Articles

Anon., 'Damansky – Land of Heroes' (Даманский – земля героев []in Russian]), *Starshina – Serzhant*, 5 (1969), pp.4–7

Anon., 'The Red Ice of the Ussuri' (Красный лед Уссури [in Russian]), *Vostok Rossii*, 10:32 (1992), pp.8–9

Burr, W., 'Sino-American Relations. 1969: The Sino-Soviet Border War and Steps Towards Rapprochement,' *Cold War History*, 1:3 (2001), pp.73–112

Danhui, Li 'Sino-Soviet Border Conflicts in 1969: Causes and Effects' [in Chinese], *Dangdai zhongguoshi yanjiu*, 3 (1996), pp.39-50.

Fridyev, V. 'A Border of Living Hearts,' (Граница живых сердец [in Russian]), *Okeanskiye vesti*, 17 (1999)

Goldstein, Lyle, 'Return to Zhenbao Island: Who Started Shooting and Why It Matters,' *The China Quarterly*, 168 (December 2001), pp.985–997.

Jun, Niu, Baijia, Zhang and others, '1966–1976: Isolation is Replaced by Openness' (1966–1976: Изоляция сменяется открытостью [in Russian]), *Mirovye znaniya*, 13:1 July (2006), pp.19-22 (translated from Chinese by D.V. Kiselev)

Koleshnya, M.I. 'Damansky Island, 1969' (Остров Даманский, год 1969 [in Russian]), *Rossiya i ATR*, 2 (1999), pp.86–87.

Kuisong, Yang, 'The Sino-Soviet Border Clash of 1969: From Zhenbao Island to Sino-American Rapprochement,' *Cold War History*, 1:1 (2000), pp.21–53

Mizhou, Hui 'Sino-Soviet Battles on the Border' (Русско-китайские побоища на границе [in Russian]), *Kempo*, 1997, No.2 (34), pp.5–6

Ostermann, S.F., "East German Documents on the Sino-Soviet Border Conflict, 1969," *The Cold War in Asia, Cold War International History Project Bulletin*, Issues 6–7 (1995/96), pp.186–193

Pankov, Yu. and Ryskin, A., 'Secret Island: What Happened on Damansky in March 1969?' (Таинственный остров: Что происходило на Даманском в марте 1969? [in Russian]), *Molodoy Dalnevostochnik*, 15 December 1990

Ryabushkin, D.S., 'Damansky Island, 2 March 1969' (Остров Даманский, 2 Марта 1969 года [in Russian]), *Voprosy istorii*, 5 (2004), pp.148–152

Ryabushkin, D.S., 'How Did the Events on Damansky Island End' (Чем завершилось события на острове Даманском [in Russian]), *Voprosy istorii*, 12 (2005), pp. 168–170

Ryabushkin, D.S., 'It Was on Damanskii Island,' *The Journal of Slavic Military Studies*, 31:4 (2018), pp.1–16

Ryabushkin, D.S., 'The Myths of Damanskii Island (1969),' *The Journal of Slavic Military Studies*, 16:3 (2003), pp.149–172

Ryabushkin, D.S., 'New Documents on the Sino-Soviet Ussuri Border Clashes,' *Eurasia Border Review*, 3 (2012), pp.161–174

Ryabushkin, D.S., 'What They Fought with on Damanskii Island,' *The Journal of Slavic Military Studies*, 19 (2006), pp.149–166

Ryabushkin, D.S., and Pavliuk, V.D., 'Soviet Artillery in the Battles for Damanskii Island,' *The Journal of Slavic Military Studies*, 20:1 (2007), pp.121–134

Vashchenko, G.T., 'Damansky: (History of the Origin of the Name Damansky Island. About Engineer S.I. Damansky)' (Даманский: (История происхождения назв. о-ва Даманский. Об инженере С.И. Даманском)[in Russian]), *Suvorovskii natisk*, 11 August 1998, p.6

Verlin, Ye, 'For Generations to Come' (На поколения вперед [in Russian]), *Ekspert*, No. 27:238 (2000), p.36

Pamphlets

Anon., 'Down with the New Tsars!,' Foreign Languages Press, Peking, 1969

Internet Sites

Anon., 'Border Conflicts and Disputes' (Приграничные конфликты и споры [in Russian]) <http://magazines.russ.ru/oz/2002/6/2002_06_27.html> (date accessed: 6 September 2020)

Anon., 'The Dulaty Operation' (Дулатинская операция [in Russian]), <https://pikabu.ru/story/dulatinskaya_operatsiya_6429090> (date accessed: 4 October 2020)

Anon., 'Border Conflicts and Disputes' (fragment published in the Journal *Fatherland Notes* (Пограничные конфликты и споры <фрагмент>, опубликовано в журнале *Отечественные записки* [in Russian]), No. 6 (2002) <http://magazines.russ.ru/oz/2002/6/2002_06_27.html> (date accessed: 4 October 2020)

Anon., 'From the History of a Great Friendship' (Из истории великой дружбы [in Russian]), *Kommersant-Vlast*, 8:309 (1999), pp.10–14. <https://www.kommersant.ru/doc/15227> (date accessed: 6 September 2020)

Department of State. Memorandum of Conversation, August 18, 1969, <https://nsarchive2.gwu.edu/NSAEBB/NSAEBB49/sino.sov.10.pdf> (date accessed: 19 September 2020).

Khrushchev, Nikita *Time, People, Power* (Время. Люди. Власть [in Russian]) <http://www.hrono.ru/libris/lib_h/hrush50.html> (date accessed: 7 September 2020)

Note of Ministry of Foreign Affairs of China, 2 March 1960 <https://books.google.com/books?id=jH3zAAAAMAAJ&pg=PA174&lpg=PA174&dq=Note+of+Ministry+of+Foreign+Affairs+of+China+2+March+1969&source=bl&ots=7qF39zRpPR&sig=ACfU3U3L9kmkzlz9YMcHL7uWUOBxUB3W4Q&hl=en&sa=X&ved=2ahUKEwjYoIa3rPnoAhUK0qYKHfoqBc4Q6AEwAXoECAoQAQ#v=onepage&q=Noteof%20Ministry%20of%20Foreign%20Affairs%20of%20China%202%20March%201969&f=false> (date accessed: 26 September 2020)

Plugatarev, I., 'Chinese Glory of Damansky Island' (Китайская слава острова Даманский [in Russian]), *Nezavisimoye voyennoye obozreniye*, 27 March 2009 (<http://nvo.ng.ru/realty/2009-03-27/10_damanskiy.html> (date accessed: 24 September 2020)).

Secretary of State. Memorandum for the President. Possibility of a Soviet Strike against Chinese Nuclear Facilities. September 10, 1969. <https://nsarchive2.gwu.edu/NSAEBB/NSAEBB49/sino.sov.19.pdf> (date accessed: 19 September 2020)

Xinren, Mao, 'Truth and Fiction about the Border Conflict on Damansky Island: the USSR and China Had to Pay Dearly' (Правда и вымысел о пограничном конфликте на острове Даманский: СССР и Китаю пришлось дорого заплатить [in Russian]) <https://inosmi.ru/social/20190317/244762270.html> (date accessed: 30 September 2020)

<http://asiapacific.narod.ru> (date accessed: 10 September 2019)

<http://citynews.tula.ru/baz/news/tk/tk020613/tk12_1.html> (date accessed: 12 June 2018)

<http://elite-soldiers.by.ru/istor8.htm> (date accessed: 1 April 2019)

<http://extend.hk.hi.cn/~daikang/junshi/zbdz.htm> (date accessed: 12 August 2019)

<http://nbp.gok.ru/Limonka/178_12_2.htm> (date accessed: 16 September 2015)

<http://wemedia.ifeng.com/49968791/wemedia.shtml> (date accessed: 12 August 2019).

<http://www.damanski-zhenbao.ru> (date accessed: 17 March 2015)

<http://www.damanski-zhenbao.ru/files/arhi-17-rus.doc> (date accessed: 27 March 2015)

<http://www.gwu.edu/nsarchiv/NSAEBB/NSAEBB49> (date accessed: 19 September 2020)

<http://www.khabenergo.ru/rus/news/press_17-03.html> (date accessed: 11 September 2020)

<http://www.maoism.ru> (date accessed: 2 August 2019)

< https://rikabu.ru/story/dulatinskaya_operatsiya_6429090> (date accessed: 16 May 2020)

<http://www.russ-chinfrien.narod.ru> (date accessed: 6 September 2020)

<https://www.scmp.com/news/china/diplomacy/article/30911611/why-russias-vladivostok-celebration-prompted-nationalist> (date accessed: 10 July 2020)

<www.fmprc.gov.cn> (date accessed: 15 June 2018)

NOTES

Chapter 1

1 Anon., *Collection of Treaties between Russia and Other States, 1856-1917* (Собрник договоров России с другими государствами. 1856-1917 [in Russian]) (Moscow: Gosudarstvennoe izdatel'stvo politicheskoi literatury, 1952); <http://www.russ-chinfrien.narod.ru> (date accessed: 6 September 2020).

2 *Collection of Treaties.*

3 Authors' note: the middle of a river and the main channel are not always one and the same. The structure of rocks lying on the bottom of a river is very important, inasmuch as the water heads toward where the ground is weakest. Another reason is the rotation of the Earth around its axis, as a result of which all rivers in the Northern Hemisphere have a steep right bank and a gently sloping left bank (vice versa in the Southern Hemisphere). The full flow of a river in some years and its shallowness in others, etc. are important. Furthermore, if hydrological work is done on a river, then it can move anywhere. Unpredictability and tendency to change course are general characteristic of Far Eastern rivers.

4 Anon., 'Border Conflicts and Disputes' (Приграничные конфликты и споры [in Russian]) <http://magazines.russ.ru/oz/2002/6/2002_06_27.html> (date accessed: 6 September 2020).

5 Anon., 'From the History of a Great Friendship' (Из истории великой дружбы [in Russian]), *Kommersant-Vlast'*, 8:309 (1999), pp.10–14. <https://www.kommersant.ru/doc/15227> (date accessed: 6 September 2020).

6 Now the Border Service of the Federal Security Service of the Russian Federation.

7 Anon., *Russian Border Troops in Wars and Military Conflicts of the 20*th *Century* (Пограничные войска в войнах и вооруженных конфликтах XX века [in Russian]) (Moscow: Granitsa, 2000), Chapter VIII. <https://royallib.com/read/kollektiv_avtorov/pogranichnie_voyska_rossii_v_voynah_i_voorugennih_konfliktah_xx_v.html#1610829> (date accessed: 6 September 2020)

8 Translator's note: There is not a one-to-one correspondence between the Russian terms and US terms for the ranks of generals. For example, Russian general major [генерал-майор] is a one-star general, while the US major general is a two-star general. To avoid confusion, the Russian variants will be used throughout this book: general major (equivalent to US brigadier general), general lieutenant (equivalent to US major general), general colonel (equivalent to US lieutenant general), general of the army (equivalent to US general), and marshal of the Soviet Union (equivalent to US general of the army).

9 Yu.M. Galenovich, *Russia and China in the 20*th *Century: The Border* (Россия и Китай в XX веке: граница [in Russian]) (Moscow: Izograf, 2001), pp.27–31, 39.

10 *Russia and China in the 20th Century*, pp.118–199.

11 *Pravda*, 14 June 1969. The full text of this announcement is given in Appendix I, at the end of Vol. 2.

12 G.T. Vashchenko, 'Damansky: (History of the Origin of the Name Damansky Island. About Engineer S.I. Damansky)' (Даманский: (История происхождения назв. о-ва Даманский. Об инженере С.И. Даманском))[in Russian]), *Suvorovskii natisk*, 11 August 1998, p.6.

13 Authors' note: Often this detachment was called the Iman Detachment, after the location of the command. The town of Iman now bears a different name – Dalnerechensk.

14 For more detailed information about Senior Lieutenant Strelnikov, see Chapter 4.

15 Authors' note: At the time this book was written, Koleshnya lived in Vladivostok. A lieutenant colonel in the reserves, he was awarded the Order of the Red Star for his participation in the events on Damansky Island.

Chapter 2

1 From Mao Zedong's second article regarding the open letter of the Central Committee of the CPSU, *The People's Daily*, 13 September 1963.

2 *New China*, 1964 (12), Peking.

3 *Rossisskaya gazeta*, 6 October 2011 (No. 5600).

4 Nikita Khrushev, *Time, People, Power* (Время. Люди. Власть [in Russian]) <http://www.hrono.ru/libris/lib_h/hrush50.html> (date accessed: 7 September 2020).

5 D.V. Streltsov (ed.), *The Territorial Issue in the Afro-Asian World* (Территориальный вопрос в афро-азиатском мире [in Russian]) (Moscow: Aspent Press, 2013), p.100.

6 Yu. Pankov and A. Ryskin, 'What Happened on Damansky in March 1969?' (Что происходило на Даманском в марте 1969? [inRussian]), *Molodoy Dalnevostochnik*, 15 December 1990.

7 Anon., 'The Red Ice of the Ussuri' (Красный лед Уссури [in Russian]), *Vostok Rossii*, 10:32 (1992), pp.8–9.

8 M. Kholmogorov (compiler), *Heroes of Damansky Island* (Герои острова Даманский [in Russian]) (Moscow: Molodaya gvaardiya, 1969), p.20.

9 <http://www.damanski-zhenbao.ru> (date accessed: 17 March 2015).

10 V. D. Bubenin, *The Bloody Snow of Damansky* (Кровавый снег Даманского [in Russian]) (Moscow: Kuchkovo pole, 2004), p.106.

11 Hui Mizhou, 'Sino-Soviet Battles on the Border' (Русско-китайские побоища на границе [in Russian]), *Кетро*, 1997, No.2 (34), pp.5–6.

12 V.F. Belyavskaya (author-compiler), *Border Guards* (Пограничники [in Russian]) (Minsk: Publisher unknown, 1998), p.168.

13 Yu.M. Galenovich, *Russia–China: Six Treaties* (Россия–Китай: шесть договоров [in Russian]) (Moscow: Muravey, 2003), pp.98–99.

14 Yu. I. Drozdov, *Notes from a Chief of Illegal Intelligence* (Записки начальника нелагальной разведки [in Russian]) (Moscow: Olma-Press, 2000), p.83.

15 *Heroes of Damansky Island*, p.93.

16 Authors' note: Chinese sources say that on this day 28 PLA soldiers were injured.

Chapter 3

1 *Pravda*, 3 March 1969.

2 See Volume 2, Appendix II

3 Chen Zhibin and Sun Xiaozhu, *Confrontation at the Freezing Point: Record of the 1962-1969 Sino-Soviet Border Battles* (Конфронтация при замораживании: запись советско-китайской пограничной битвы с 1962 по 1969 год [in Russian, translated from Chinese]) (Beijing: International Cultural Publication Company, 1992).

4 D.S. Ryabushkin, 'How Did the Events End on Damansky Island' (Чем завершились события на острове Даманском [in Russian]), *Voprosy istorii*, 12 (2005), pp.168–170.

5 Authors' note: Chinese researching this conflict cite the following data regarding the subunits occupying positions on their riverbank: two infantry companies, four intelligence platoons, one recoilless rifle platoon, and one medium machine gun platoon.

6 Translator's note: масленица (maslenitsa): an Eastern Slavic religious and folk holiday, observed the eighth week before Eastern Orthodox Easter. It corresponds to Carnival in the West; it is the preparatory week for Lent.

7 A.A. Sabadash et al., *Transcripts of Conversations with Veterans of the War on Damansky Island V.I. Abramov, A.S. Belozerov, M.T. Vashchenko, G.A. Kuzminykh, N.I. Nikiferov, V.S. Prosvirnikov, N.I. Ruban, V.P. Fateyev, A.I. Filimonov, 2002-2003* (Стенограммы бесед с участниками конфликта на острове Даманском В.И. Абрамовым, А.С. Белсеровым, М.Т. Ващенко, Г.А. Кузминых, Н.И. Никеферовым, В.С. Просвирниковым, Н.И. Рубаном, В.П. Фатеевым, А. И. Филимоновым, 2003-2004 [in Russian]) (unpublished).

8 Authors' note: All the above-cited figures should not be considered conclusive, because even veterans of the event cite somewhat different information. For example, M.I. Koleshnya cites the following distribution of border guards per vehicle: 7 + 15 + 7. In his memoirs V.D. Bubenin states that Buinevich and 5-6 border guards were in the GAZ-69, and Strelnikov came to Damansky on the APC with 14 soldiers. See V.D. Bubenin, *The Bloody Snow of Damansky*, p.154.

9 The PLA document, of course, cites Chinese local time. This would correspond to 11:17 Soviet time.

10 <http://www.damanski-zhenbao.ru/files/arhi-17-rus.doc> (date accessed: 27 March 2015).

11 I.I. Petrov, *The Sino-Soviet Wars. The Truth about Damansky* (Советско-китайские войны. Правда о Даманском [in Russian] (Moscow: 'Eksmo': 'Yauza,' 2009), p.51.

12 M.I. Koleshnya, 'Damansky Island, 1969' (Остров Даманский, год 1969 [in Russian]), *Rossiya i ATR*, 2 (1999), pp.86–87.

13 Authors' note: At an exhibition at the Central Border Museum of the FSB RF, Kanygin's actions were described as follows: 'In the clash with the Chinese provocateurs on 2 March, he held back the onslaught of up to 40 armed Maoists, killing half of them. For personal bravery he was awarded the Order of Lenin'

14 Petrov, *The Sino-Soviet Wars*, pp.64–65.

15 Bubenin, *The Bloody Snow of Damansky*, p.162.

16 Ye.D. Leonova and V.B. Murin, *Demokrat Leonov: a Life in the Name of Duty* (Демократ Леонов: жизнь во имя долга [in Russian]) (Moscow: Granitsa, 2016), p.43.

17 P. Razmazin, *Damansky. Our Pain. Sorrow. Memory . . .* (Даманский. Наше боль. Скорбь. Память . . . [in Russian]), a project of P. Razmazin (Dalnerechensk: B.M.I., 1999), p.5.

18 Excerpt from a letter to author D.S. Ryabushkin.

19 'From the History of a Great Friendship' (date accessed: 8 September 2020).

Chapter 4

1 Bubenin, *The Bloody Snow of Damansky*, p.34.

2 Translator's note: akrikhin (mepacrine) – a yellow, crystalline immunosuppressant drug.

3 From the collection of the Dalnerechensk Museum of Historyvia V.N. Volik.

Chapter 5

1 Translator's note: the list is alphabetical according to the Cyrillic alphabet.

2 Authors' note: An asterisk following the name indicates that the soldier served at the Kulebyakiny Hills Outpost. These soldiers are singled out because in some sources the names and numbers of soldiers from this outpost who died are incorrect. Even Bubenin himself in his memoirs misnamed one of the soldiers.

3 Bubenin, *The Bloody Snow of Damansky*, p.169.

4 Authors' note: The list was provided by A.A. Sabadash, who visited the cemetery where the Chinese servicemen were buried and photographed all the graves of those who perished on Damansky.

5 I. Plugatarev, 'Chinese Glory of Damansky Island' (Китайская слава острова Даманский [in Russian]), *Nezavisimoye voyennoye obozreniye*, 27 March 2009 (http://nvo.ng.ru/realty/2009-03-27/10_damanskiy.html (date accessed: 24 September 2020)).

6 From a letter to author D.S. Ryabushkin.

Chapter 6

1 M. Kholmogorov (compiler), *Heroes of Damansky Island* (Герои острова даманский [in Russian]) (Moscow: Molodaya gvardiya, 1969), p.9. The full text is given in Appendix III at the end of Volume 2.

2 See Volume 2, Appendix IV.

3 Authors' note: A copy of the original medical certificate was first published in D.S. Ryabushkin, *Damansky Island. Border War. March 1969* (Остров Даманский. Пограничный конфликт. Март 1969 [in Russian]) (Moscow: Russkiye vityazi, 2015). An English translation first appeared in Dmitri S. Ryabushkin, 'New Documents on the Sino-Soviet Ussuri Border Clashes of 1969,' *Eurasia Border Review*, Vol. 3, Japan, Sapporo, 2012, pp.159–174. That translation has been modified here to correspond more closely to English medical terminology.

4 "Down with the New Tsars!," Foreign Languages Press, Peking, 1969

Chapter 7

1 *Peking Review*, v.12, №10 (1969), pp.5,7.

2 *Renmin Ribao*, 3 March 1969. This citation and the text itself can be found at https://books.google.com/books?id=jH3zAAAAMAAJ&pg=PA174&lpg=PA174&dq=Note+of+Ministry+of+Foreign+Affairs+of+China+2+March+1969&source=bl&ots=7qF39zRpPR&sig=ACfU3U3L9kmkzlz9YMcHL7uWUOBxUB3W4Q&hl=en&sa=X&ved=2ah UKEwjYoIa3rPno AhUK0qYKHfoqBc4Q6AEwAXoECAoQAQ#v=onepage&q=Note%20of%20Ministry%20of%20 Foreign%20Affairs%20of%20China%202%20March%201969&f=false (date accessed: 26 September 2020).

3 Yang Kuisong, 'The Sino-Soviet Border Clash of 1969: From Zhenbao Island to Sino-American Rapprochement,' *Cold War History*, 1:1 (2000), pp.21–52.

4 *Soviet Military Encyclopaedia* (Советская военная энциклопедия [in Russian]), Vol. 3 (Moscow: Voyenizdat, 1979), p.412.

5 Yang Kuisong, 'The Sino-Soviet Border Clash of 1969'.

6 Li Danhui, 'Sino-Soviet Border Conflicts in 1969: Causes and Effects' [in Chinese], *Dangdai zhongguoshi yanjiu*, 3 (1996).

7 Lyle Goldstein, 'Return to Zhenbao Island: Who Started Shooting and Why It Matters,' *The China Quarterly*, 168 (December 2001), pp.985–997

Chapter 8

1 Authors' note: The title of this chapter comes from Mikhail Bulgakov's novel *The Master and Margarita*. The sense of it is that if something is written down and read by people, then even if the manuscript is burned or disappears, it will not be lost, inasmuch as society will preserve and circulate important and valuable ideas.

2 I.I. Petrov, *The Sino-Soviet Wars. The Truth about Damansky* (Советско-китайские войны. Правда о Даманском [in Russian]) (Moscow, 'Eksmo': 'Yauza,' 2009), p.48. The remaining citations in this chapter are from Petrov's book, pp.51–54, 57–61, 70.

3 Authors' note: The Petrov mentioned here was the driver of the GAZ-69 from the Kulebyakiny Sopki outpost, not to be confused with Nikolay Petrov, the photographer who died with Senior Lieutenant Strelnikov (see Chapter 3).

Chapter 9

1 Unless otherwise indicated, all citations in this chapter have been taken from the unpublished memoirs of General Major V.T. Shchur.

2 V Lukashin, *The Heroes of Damansky* (Герои Даманского [in Russian]) (Moscow: Izvestiya, 1969), p.73.

Chapter 10

1 T. W. Robinson, *The Sino-Soviet Border Dispute: Background, Development, and the March 1969 Clashes*, Rand Corporation Research Memorandum RM-6171-PR, 1970. Unless otherwise indicated, all direct citations in this chapter come from Robinson's book. The page numbers where a citation is found in the original are given in brackets ([ ]) at the end of each citation. The original US spelling is retained. The spelling of proper names reflect Robinson's original text, and may differ from the spellings of these same names that have been used throughout this work. Punctuation in citations also reflects the punctuation in the original.

2 Hunzy, in our book.

3 The name is incorrect in Robinson's text. It should be Babansky.

4 See Chapter 3.

5 Thomas Robinson, in various authors, *The Cambridge History of China* (Cambridge University Press: Cambridge, 1992) Vol. 15: 'The People's Republic. Part 2. Revolutions within the Chinese Revolution, 1966-1982'.

6 In *The Sino-Soviet Border Dispute*, Robinson cites Hugo Portisch in the Vienna *Kurier*, translated in *Atlas*, Vol. 14, No. 3 (September 1967), pp.15–19.

7 Heilongjiang in our book.

Chapter 11

1 Li Zhisui, *Notes of a Personal Physician* (Записки личного врача [in Russian]), Book 1 (Minsk: Inter-Digest, Smolensk: TOO Ekho, 1996), p.319.

2 A.A. Brezhnev, *China: The Thorny Path to Good Neighbourliness* (Китай: тернистый путь к добрососедству [in Russian]) (Moscow: Mezhdunarodnye otnosheniya, 1998), pp.175–178.

3 Robinson, *The Sino-Soviet Border Dispute*, pp.61–62.

4 Robinson, *The Sino-Soviet Border Dispute*, pp.62–63.

5 Robinson, *The Sino-Soviet Border Dispute*, p.63.

6 Robinson, *The Sino-Soviet Border Dispute*, p.64.

7 Hui Mizhou, 'Sino-Soviet Battles on the Border,' p.5.

8 Yang Kuisong, 'The Sino-Soviet Border Clash of 1969,' p.27–28.

9 Yang Kuisong, 'The Sino-Soviet Border Clash of 1969,' p.28–29.

10 Niu Jun, Zhang Baijia, Li Danhui, Xu Yan, Liu Jianyong, and Li Qunying, '1966–1976: Isolation is Replaced by Openness' (1966–1976: Изоляция сменяется открытостью [in Russian]), *Mirovye znaniya*, 13:1 July (2006) (translated from Chinese by D.V. Kiselev).

11 Mao Xinren, 'Truth and Fiction about the Border Conflict on Damansky Island: The USSR and China Had to Pay Dearly' (Правда и вымысел о пограничном конфликте на острове Даманский: СССР и Китаю пришлось дорого заплатить [in Russian]) <https://inosmi.ru/social/20190317/244762270.html> (date accessed: 30 September 2020).

Chapter 12

1 S.F. Ostermann, "East German Documents on the Sino-Soviet Border Conflict, 1969," *The Cold War in Asia, Cold War International History Project Bulletin*, Issues 6–7 (1995/96), pp.186–193.

2 *Izvestiya*, 8 March 1969.

3 The examples were taken from *Heroes of Damansky Island*.

4 'Down with the New Tsars!' (Foreign Languages Press: Peking, 1969). This pamphlet copied the full text of the editorial from *The People's Daily* and *The People's Liberation Army Daily*, translated it into English, and published it in the pamphlet. This citation is taken from that English translation of the original editorial.

5 Ostermann, 'East German Documents on the Sino-Soviet Border Conflict.'

6 See Volume 2, Appendix IV.

ABOUT THE AUTHORS

Dmitry Ryabushkin

Born in the USSR, Dr. of Physics and Mathematics, Associate Professor at the Crimean Federal University named after V.I. Vernadsky. He has published five monographs and more than 50 articles in the field of physics, teaching methods, and problems of university education in Russia. He has been studying the subject of the Sino-Soviet border war since 2000. He has published four monographs on this theme: *The Myth of Damansky* [*Мифы Даманского*] in 2004; *Damansky Island. The Border Conflict. March 1969* [*Остров Даманский. Пограничный конфликт. Март 1969 года*] in 2015; *It Was on Damansky* [*Это было на Даманском*] in 2019; and *The Sino-Soviet Border Conflict of 1969* [*Советско-китайский пограничный конфликт 1969 года*] in 2020 (the original Russian-language version of this translation), as well as more than 10 articles on this subject in scholarly journals in Russia, the US, and Japan. He is recognized in Russia as one of the most objective and informative experts in the field of the history of the 1969 Sino-Soviet border conflict. This is his first publication for Helion.

Harold Orenstein

Born in the US. Received his MA and PhD in Slavic Languages from The Ohio State University. Retired since 2009 from US government service, during his 31-year career he was a translator-analyst for the Foreign Research Division of the Library of Congress; taught Russian at the US Army Russian Institute; worked as a translator, editor, and analyst for the Foreign Military Studies Office (formerly the Soviet Army Studies Office) at Fort Leavenworth, Kansas; served as a military-political analyst for Central and East European affairs at SHAPE (NATO's military branch); and served as a military analyst specialising in US joint and multinational doctrine for the Combined Arms Doctrine Directorate at Fort Leavenworth, Kansas. He has served as the documents editor of *The Journal of Slavic Military Studies* since its founding in 1988, translating numerous Russian-language articles. His publications include the translation of seven USSR General Staff studies dealing with Soviet Army operations on the Eastern Front during the Second World War; *The Evolution of Soviet Operational Art*; *Captured Soviet Generals: The Fate of Soviet Generals Captured by the Germans*; and, most recently (2017), *The Price of Victory: The Red Army's Casualties in the Great Patriotic War.*